T0123252

Spark!

Spark!

Ignite the leader in you

Ken Chapman

iUniverse

iUniverse books may be ordered through booksellers or by contacting:

iUniverse
1663 Liberty Drive
Bloomington, IN 47403
www.iuniverse.com
1-800-Authors (1-800-288-4677)

ISBN: 978-1-5320-3420-6 (sc)
ISBN: 978-1-5320-3418-3 (hc)
ISBN: 978-1-5320-3419-0 (e)

Library of Congress Control Number: 2017914978

Print information available on the last page.

iUniverse rev. date: 11/08/2017

Also by Ken Chapman

The Respectable Fish 1995
The Leader's Code 1999, 2003, 2014
Personality: Making the Most of It 2002
Small Town Graces 2003
The Shoulders of Giants 2005 Anthony
James and Ken Chapman

DEDICATION

For
Jeremiah . Emma . Rahel . Lorena . John

CONTENTS

Leadership

Growth

Faith

One- Minute Lessons

ACKNOWLEDGEMENTS

As is true of most things in life, what follows is the product of many. This book is possible because of the knowledge, skill, wisdom, and goodwill of others. I stand on the twin shoulders of candor and care. Friends, colleagues, and family have provided honest critique along with encouragement and inspiration.

My special thanks to Whitney Tate, Grace Shim, Rhonda Chapman, Jean Graham, Christy Beem, and Deb Miller. They have made this collection of stories better and more readable than they would have been.

For my teachers, professors and mentors—from grade school on, I am thankful as well. I could easily cite more names and I could say more; however, in deference to brevity, I offer the following: As this book goes to press, I am confirmed in my belief that life has always been unfair to me. I have *never* received what I deserved. I have always received far more.

Ken Chapman
Autumn 2017

PREFACE/INTRODUCTION

Storytelling is at the center of the human experience. It has been, and remains, a much-loved source of entertainment. While a well-told story is certainly great entertainment, it is much more than just entertainment. Stories are a time-honored way of transmitting experience and wisdom across cultures and time. We remember stories long after they are told. They touch our hearts and minds. And, they help children and adults alike get a handle on right and wrong, better and best. As a result, we avoid the mistakes of the past. We are enabled to grow toward a more hopeful future. It is in the reading and sharing of stories we learn to better tell *our story*. Our lives are a series of events—stories! In telling *our story* we make a contribution to the great reservoir of human experience.

It is my hope *Spark!* will find a welcome place in this long tradition of wisdom and entertainment. May it spark your imagination and brighten your spirit. May *Spark* entertain you as you make your contribution to the long history of well-told stories.

Consider a *Spark!* story as a platform for discussing an important issue in the workplace. Share a story to cheer up a friend. Read the stories to children and grandchildren. Tell one or more of them in your own words, even better, share your own stories.

Life

Spark!

SIMPLE SOLUTIONS

Dr. Thomas Edison's fame had become international. He was advised to have scientists come to his lab and help him understand *scientifically* why his inventions had worked. Edison consented to do so, even though he did not think much of the idea. As a result, a brilliant research scientist from Germany came to Edison's lab to explain to him the principles behind Edison's innovations. While the scientist was visiting the lab, Edison handed the man a globe that had been twisted into a gourd-like shape and said, "Give me the cubic content of this."

Weeks passed and eventually, Edison sought out the man to ask him why he had not replied. The scientist began to give him a lengthy explanation about the difficulties of solving such a problem with higher mathematics. Edison then picked up the globe, took it to a nearby sink, and filled it with water. He poured the water into a measuring tube, and holding up the tube he said, "This is the cubic content."

The solutions to most problems are probably far simpler than we think they might be. They usually stem from an understanding of basic principles, the *whys* of life. If we ask why, we will often find the answer, but we must be willing to take the answers that we find and use them for good. Edison may not have understood the scientific principles behind his inventions, but he used his inventions for the benefit of others. Edison knew it is not our scientific knowledge that inspires others to follow us, but rather our willingness to take the answers we find and use them for good.

A SMALL TOWN MERCHANT

The founder of Wal-Mart, Sam Walton, has been called many things including enemy of small-town America and destroyer of main-street merchants. "Quite a few small stores have gone out of business during the time of Wal-Mart's growth," conceded Walton. "Some people have tried to turn it into this big controversy, sort of a save the small-town merchant's deal like they were whales or whooping cranes or something." The truth is Walton was a small-town main street merchant of the type he is criticized for displacing. The only difference is he was an excellent innovator who was able to solve problems and change rather than risk going out of business.

Sam Walton was born in Kingfish, Oklahoma, and grew up in Columbia, Missouri. He demonstrated leadership in high school when he was elected student body president and led his football team to an undefeated season and state championship as its quarterback. He then performed the same feat with the basketball team as its five-foot, nine-inch floor leader. After graduating from college and working for a few years, Walton served in the Army during World War II. When he got out, he selected a career in retail, the field he loved and along with his wife, picked the small town of Bentonville, Arkansas, in which to live. That is where they opened a Walton's Five and Dime Store. The business did well partly because of Walton's hustle. But most of all, the store prospered because he demonstrated foresight in making his store self-service, a new concept at the time. He worked hard and continued to expand. By 1960, he had fifteen stores, but that was also about the time when competitor, Herb Gibson brought discount stores into Northwest Arkansas. They competed directly with Walton's Variety Stores. "We really had only two choices," said Walton, "stay in the variety store business and be hit hard by the discounting wave or open a discount store. So I started running all over the country studying the concept. We opened Wal-Mart No. 1 on July 2, 1962, in Rogers, Arkansas, right down the road from Bentonville."

Walton soon added additional stores. His Wal-Mart chain was small compared to some others that began around the same time: K-Mart, Target, and Woolco. But Wal-Mart was going strong and that led to the next problem. Walton realized he needed to improve the stores' planning and distribution. He and his people solved the problem by creating central distribution centers. That, along with computerization, allowed them to order in bulk, keep track of each store's needs, and distribute to them quickly and efficiently. And when the outlay for new equipment and buildings for the new distribution center created a heavy debt load, it was merely another problem to be solved. Walton did it by taking the company public in 1970.

When Sam Walton died in 1992, the company operated more than seventeen hundred stores in forty-two states and Mexico. Sam Walton, the small-town variety store owner, had become America's number one retailer.

HOLIDAY INN

It was in 1951 that a Memphis businessman named Kemmons Wilson took his family on a vacation to Washington, D.C. It was there he learned about the state of hotel lodging in the United States. Motels had sprung up all over the country since the 1920s. Some were nice family places, others rented beds by the hour. The problem was the traveler did not know which he would find. "You never could tell what you were getting," Wilson recalls later. "Some of the places were too squalid for words and they all charged extra for children. They made my Scottish blood boil."

Wilson, who had five children, found traveling expenses daunting. Hotels charged four to six dollars a night for a room plus two dollars extra per child. It would triple the bill. Most people would have complained and then forgotten about it. But Wilson, always the initiator, decided to take action and to do something about it. "Let's go home and start a chain of family hotels," he said to his wife. "Hotels with a name you can trust." His goal was to build four hundred hotels. His wife just laughed.

When Wilson returned to Memphis, he hired a draftsman to help him design his first hotel. He wanted it to be clean, simple, and predictable. He wanted it to have all the things he and his family had missed such as a television in every room and a pool. The next year he opened his first hotel on the outskirts of Memphis. Its name flashed out from a huge fifty-three-foot tall sign. It was called *The Holiday Inn.*

It took Wilson longer than he expected to reach four hundred hotels. By 1959, he had one hundred, but then he decided to franchise them and that boosted the openings. By 1964, there were five hundred Holiday Inns; in 1968, there were one thousand; and by 1972, a Holiday Inn opened somewhere in the world every seventy-two hours.

THE GREEN PORSCHE

Once upon a time a handyman rang a doorbell in a well-to-do neighborhood. Much to his surprise, the handyman was greeted warmly by the lady who opened the door. She stated she was glad to see him because she had been hoping to find someone to do some painting.

"Do you see that bucket of green paint there beside the doorstep?" she asked.

"Yes," the man replied.

"Well, I've been looking for someone to paint my porch. If you'll just go around back and put a coat of paint on it, I would appreciate it."

The man replied, "Thank you," and went to work.

A couple of hours later, he rang the doorbell again and announced the job was complete.

She thanked him and said, "Well, let's take a look."

So they went around back and the lady discovered that the man had, in fact, put a nice coat of green paint on her Porsche. When questioned, the man explained, "Well, I thought you said to paint your Porsche, I didn't realize you meant porch."

ROSALIE

During the National Spelling Bee in Washington, D.C., eleven-year-old Rosalie Elliott, a champion from South Carolina, was asked to spell the word, "avowal." Her soft Southern accent made it difficult for the judges to determine if she had used an "a" or an "e" in the last syllable of the word. The judges deliberated for several minutes and listened to tape playbacks. Still they could not determine which letter had been used. Finally, the chief judge asked Rosalie, "Was the letter an a or an e?"

Rosalie knew by now the correct spelling of the word and realized she had misspelled it. If she lied, she could continue. If she told the truth, she would lose. While some may have chosen to win at any cost, Rosalie's conscience guided her response. Without hesitation, Rosalie replied that she had misspelled the word and had used an "e." As she walked from the stage, the entire audience stood and applauded her honesty.

It was clear the audience felt Rosalie had won something bigger than a spelling bee—the respect and admiration of everyone present.

BEGINNING WITH THE END IN MIND

In 1977, twelve-year-old Michael sat on a beach along the Gulf of Mexico. Painstakingly, he put together a trot line, a maze of ropes to which several fish hooks can be attached. Meanwhile, his parents and two brothers were busy fishing. "You're wasting your time," they advised him, "Grab a pole and join in the fun."

Undaunted, Michael kept working at his tedious task, even though his family considered it a waste of time. At dinnertime when everyone else was ready to call it a day, Michael cast his trot line far into the water. He then anchored it to a stick he had plunged deep into the sand. During dinner, his family teased him about coming away from the day's fishing empty handed. But after dinner, when Michael reeled in his trot line, there were more fish on it than the entire family had caught.

Michael Dell got his start in high school when he bought his first computer and took it apart to figure out how it worked. Seventeen years later, his patient persistence had taken him from teen to tycoon. He became the fourth largest manufacturer of personal computers in the United States and the youngest man ever to head a Fortune 500 corporation.

Michael believed in what he was doing. Whether he was fishing or building computers, he always began with the end in mind.

KINDNESS RETURNS

Many years ago, an elderly man and his wife entered the lobby of a small Philadelphia hotel. "Every guest room is taken," the clerk said, but then added, "I can't send a nice couple like you out into the rain, though. Would you be willing to sleep in my room?"

The next morning, the elderly man said to the clerk, "You are the kind of man who should be the boss of the best hotel in the United States. Maybe someday, I'll build one for you." The clerk laughed and forgot about the incident.

Two years later, however, he received a letter containing a round trip ticket to New York and a request that he be the guest of the elderly couple. Once in New York, the old man led the clerk to the corner of Fifth Avenue and Thirty-Fourth Street where he pointed to an incredible new building and declared, "That is the hotel I have just built for you to manage." The young man, George C. Boldt, accepted the offer of William Waldorf Astor to become the manager of the original Waldorf Astoria Hotel.

Over the next twenty-three years George Boldt remained faithful to William Waldorf Astor's vision of hospitality and comfort. And Boldt's efforts would come to define the essence of a great "home away from home."

PAIN BRINGS A PURPOSE

One day, Bea Salazar sat looking at a bottle of painkillers thinking of suicide. She was a single mother of five, whose husband had abandoned the family. Bea had been disabled in a factory accident. Her pelvis and back were so badly injured she could no longer work. She was in terrible pain, financially broke, and full of despair. Then she heard a knock on her door. It was the counselor Bea had been seeing. And to this day, Bea believes God sent this special visitor.

With her counselor's help, Bea began to live again, painfully regaining control of her life and looking for its meaning. That meaning appeared in a most unexpected way. While taking out the garbage, Bea heard a noise in her dumpster. Inside, she found a small boy eating a piece of dirty bread. She took him home and fed him. But soon, six more children showed up asking for food; thirteen more the next day. It seemed there were many kids in the neighborhood whose parents left them alone with nothing to eat all day. Bea suddenly realized she had found her mission. God had saved her life, "because he needs me to take care of these children."

She pleaded for donations from agencies and churches and in 1990, she formed "Bea's Kids," a nonprofit organization. Now she and her staff feed 150 kids each day and offer tutoring, clothes, medical aid, and more. Some days, Bea can hardly walk due to her injuries, but she gets out of bed to greet the children who come to her. "They give me a purpose, in fact, they have given me much more than I have ever given them."

THE UGLIEST MAN

President Abraham Lincoln had a disarming and engaging ability to laugh at himself, especially his own physical appearance. When Senator Stephen A. Douglas called him a "two-faced man," Lincoln responded, "I leave it to my audience. If I had another face, do you think I would wear this one?"

Another time, he told a group of editors about meeting a woman riding on horseback in the woods. She looked at me intently and said, "I do believe you are the ugliest man I ever saw."

Lincoln responded, "Madam, you are probably right, but I can't help it."

"No," she said, "but you might stay home."

Although his likeness is widely recognized, Lincoln is not known primarily for his appearance. He is remembered for his courageous efforts to restore the Union and abolish slavery. He is often held up as an example of remarkable patience, determination, compassion, and selflessness. These inner qualities are what mark Lincoln as one of America's greatest presidents.

So much is made in our culture today of outward appearance and material possessions. As with President Lincoln, it is virtuous inner qualities which create a lasting legacy.

TOP TEN FAILURES

Guess these top ten failures of all time [answers next page].

10. The engineer who neglected to design a reverse gear in the first car he manufactured

9. The group turned down by Decca Records because "guitars are on their way out"

8. The illustrator told by his newspaper editor to pursue another line of work

7. The skinny kid who hated the way he looked and was always being beat up by bullies

6. The seriously ill, deeply in debt composer, who in desperation wrote an oratorio in a few hours

5. The obese, deformed eccentric who became a reclusive thinker

4. The orchestra conductor and composer, who made his greatest contributions after becoming deaf

3. The politician who lost his first seven elections

2. The boy everyone thought was mute because his stutter was so bad he never spoke until he was a teenager

1. The woman born deaf and blind, who became a great writer and philanthropist and once said, "I thank God for my handicaps."

ANSWERS

10. Henry Ford
9. The Beatles
8. Walt Disney
7. Charles Atlas
6. George Frederick Handel [The Messiah]
5. Socrates
4. Ludwig Von Beethoven
3. Abraham Lincoln
2. James Earl Jones
1. Helen Keller

Our greatest disappointments can produce our greatest successes. It is our attitudes toward those disappointments which make all the difference.

BLIND AMBITION

Charlie Boswell, a native Alabamian, was well known in the golf world. Over and beyond his lifetime he inspired thousands of people to rise above circumstances and live more hopeful lives. Charlie was blinded during World War II while rescuing his friend from a tank that was under fire. He was a great athlete before his accident and as testimony to his talent and determination, he decided to try a brand-new sport, a sport he never imagined playing even with his eyesight. That sport is golf.

Through determination and a deep love for the game, he became the National Blind Golf Champion. He won that honor thirteen times. One of his heroes was the great golfer, Ben Hogan. So, it truly was an honor for Charlie to win the Ben Hogan Award in 1958. Upon meeting Ben Hogan, Charlie was awe struck and stated that he had one wish and it was to have one round of golf with the great Ben Hogan.

Mr. Hogan agreed that playing a round together would be an honor for him as well. Hogan had heard about Charlie's accomplishments and truly admired his skills. "Would you like to play for money, Mr. Hogan?" asked Charlie.

"I can't play you for money. It would be unfair," said Mr. Hogan.

"Aw, come on Mr. Hogan, a thousand dollars a hole?"

"I can't. What would people think of me taking advantage of you and your circumstance," replied the great golfer.

"Chicken, Mr. Hogan?"

"Okay," blurted the frustrated Hogan. "But I am going to play my best."

"I wouldn't expect anything else," said the confident Boswell.

"You're on, Mr. Boswell. You name the time and place."

A very self-assured Charlie Boswell responded, "Ten o'clock tonight."

BOBBY JONES

Bobby Jones, one of golf's greatest players, was only five years old when he first swung a golf club. By the age of twelve, he was winning club tournaments. His hot temper was also earning him the nickname, "Club Thrower."

During this time, Jones became friends with a part-time pro shop employee, Grandpa Bart. In his day, Bart had been an excellent golfer and had retired when arthritis crippled his hands. When Bobby lost the national amateur tournament at the age of fourteen, Bart said, "Bobby, you are good enough to win that tournament, but you'll never win until you can control that temper of yours. You miss a shot, you get upset, and then you lose."

Bobby knew Grandpa Bart was right, and he became determined to improve not his golf swing, but his mood swing. When Bobby won a major tournament at age twenty-one, Grandpa Bart commented, "Bobby was fourteen when he mastered the game of golf, but he was twenty-one when he mastered himself."

LIVING EXAMPLE

Reporters and city officials gathered at a Chicago railroad station on an autumn afternoon in 1953. The person they were awaiting was the winner of the 1952 Nobel Peace Prize. A few minutes after the train came to a stop, a giant of a man, six feet, four inches, with bushy hair and a large mustache stepped from the train. Cameras flashed. City officials approached him with hands outstretched. Various people began telling him how honored they were to have him in their city.

The man politely thanked them and then, looking over their heads, asked if he could be excused for a moment. He quickly walked through the crowd until he reached the side of an elderly black woman struggling with two large suitcases. He picked up the bags and with a smile, escorted the woman to a bus. After helping her aboard, he wished her a safe journey. As he turned to the greeting party, he apologized, "Sorry to have kept you waiting."

The man was Dr. Albert Schweitzer, the famous medical missionary who had spent his life helping the people of central Africa. In response to Schweitzer's action, one member of the reception committee said with great admiration to the reporter standing next to him, "That's the first time I ever saw a sermon walking."

THE ENVELOPE

This is a true story told by a woman named Judith Garnen who lives in Tacoma, Washington. The story goes as follows:

It all began because my husband Mike hated Christmas. Oh, not the true meaning of Christmas, but the commercial aspects of it: over spending, the frantic running around at the last minute to get a tie for this one or perfume for that one, the gifts given in desperation because you couldn't think of anything else.

Knowing he felt this way, I decided one year to bypass the usual shirts, sweaters, ties, and so forth. I reached for something special just for Mike. The inspiration came in an unusual way. Our son, Kevin, was twelve that year and was wrestling at the junior level at the school he attended. Shortly before Christmas, there was a non-league match against a team sponsored by an inner-city church comprised of mostly black youth. These youngsters dressed in sneakers so ragged that shoe strings seemed to be the only thing holding them together. They presented a sharp contrast to our boys in their spiffy blue and gold uniforms and sparkling wrestling shoes. As the match began, I was alarmed to see that the other team was wrestling without head gear, a kind of light helmet designed to protect a wrestler's ears. It was a luxury the rag-tag team obviously could not afford.

My son's team won the match, taking every weight class. As each of these boys from the church-sponsored team got up from the mat, he swaggered away in his tatters with false bravado, a kind of street pride that could not acknowledge defeat.

Mike, seated beside me, shook his head sadly, "I wish just one of them could have won. They have a lot of potential, but losing like this could take the heart right out of them."

Mike loved kids, all kids and he knew them, having coached Little League football, baseball, and soccer. That is when the idea for this present came to me. That afternoon, I went to a local sporting goods store and bought an assortment of wrestling headgear and shoes and sent them anonymously to the inner-city church. On Christmas Eve, I placed the envelope on the tree, the note inside telling Mike what I had done and that this was his gift from me. The smile was the brightest thing about Christmas that year and in succeeding years. For each Christmas, I followed the tradition. One year I sent a group of mentally handicapped youngsters to a hockey game. Another year, a check was sent to a pair of elderly brothers whose home had been burned to the ground the week before Christmas, and so on.

The envelope became the highlight of our Christmas. It was always the last thing opened on Christmas morning and our children, ignoring their new toys, would stand with wide-eyed anticipation as their dad lifted the envelope from the tree to reveal its contents. As the children grew, the toys gave way to more practical presents, but the envelope never lost its allure.

The story does not end there. We lost Mike last year due to cancer. When Christmas rolled around, I was still so wrapped in grief that I barely got the tree up. But Christmas Eve found me placing an envelope on the tree, and in the morning it was joined by three more. Each of our children, unbeknownst to me, had placed an envelope on the tree for their dad. Mike's spirit, like the Christmas spirit, will always be with us.

A GOOD PLACE TO LIVE

Every now and then, I find myself overhearing a conversation in which someone asserts the United States is really not such a great nation. I suppose if you want to look at what this nation has done wrong, you can make the argument, as is true with most nations, we have made mistakes. And yet, when I hear people suggest this is not such a great nation, I think about stories like the one I read recently, written by an eighty-four-year-old retired math professor at the University of Michigan. On June 25, 1950, this professor, now living in the United States, was a colonel in the Army of the Republic of [South] Korea, his name—Colonel Hoang Lee.

Col. Lee was a young officer in the South Korean Army who found himself in a very difficult position. As the North Koreans crossed the 38th Parallel in their invasion of South Korea, he and his soldiers conducted one of the most difficult military maneuvers any army can undertake. They fought and fell back, fought and fell back, fought and fell back. They were doing everything they could in order to make it possible for the South Korean Nation to survive. He was, of course, buying time for more reinforcements to join him. More than that, he and his men were buying time in the hope that the American Army would come to their aid.

As they fought and fell back, more than fifty hours passed and during those hours, Col. Lee and his men had no sleep and little to eat. Finally, after fifty hours of fighting and falling back, physically and mentally exhausted Col. Lee could barely focus his eyes, he looked up to see an American Army officer approaching. He would come to know this officer as Lieutenant Colonel Harry McCaffrey.

Harry McCaffrey was the commander of the Army's 32nd Infantry. As McCaffrey walked up to Col. Lee, Col. Lee pulled all of his strength together to report what he could to Lt. Col. McCaffrey concerning what had taken place. In his struggle to deal with the American officer as one soldier to another, all that he could say was, "We are exhausted. We have been fighting and falling back, fighting and falling back." At this point, he fell forward, not quite fainting, but so exhausted that he could barely stand. The American officer, McCaffrey, and another soldier caught Col. Lee and helped him regain his footing. Realizing how exhausted he was and in response to his comment that they had been fighting and falling back, Lt. Col. Harry McCaffrey, from Corpus Christi, Texas, said to the South Korean officer, "Sir, I am here under the orders of the President of the United States and I assure you that we will fight with you—together, we will fall back no more."

Lt. Col. McCaffrey turned out to be as good as his word because the integrity of the South Korean Nation was restored through the efforts of the United States Armed Forces. Col. Hoang Lee would leave South Korea in the late 1950s after his nation was safe and secure. He would pursue doctoral studies in the United States and spend many years teaching at an American university. But Col. Lee, in the telling of his story, relates that every time he sees an American flag, he sees the face of Harry McCaffrey who told him in the most desperate moment of his life and that of his nation's life, "We will fight with you—together, we will fall back no more."

Just a little something to keep in mind, when you hear someone suggest this is not such a great nation or such a great place to live.

SEEDS AND DEEDS

A man was walking to church one night when he encountered four boys loitering on the street corner. He invited them to go to the service with him. They did and each of the boys also agreed to return to church with him the next Sunday. They became the nucleus of a Sunday school class the man began to teach.

Years later, a group of the man's friends decided to contact the four boys to see what had happened in their lives. Once contacted, the boys were invited to write a special birthday letter to their former teacher. The letters were to be read at a surprise party. Their letters revealed one of them had become a missionary to China, one was the president of a federal reserve bank, one was the private secretary to President Herbert Hoover, and the fourth was President Herbert Hoover, himself.

If you were to hold a handful of seeds in your hand, you could not begin to predict which of the seeds might actually sprout and produce a giant tree. It is amazing such a large tree might grow from such a small seed. The only way to know which seeds have trees hidden inside is to plant them. When acts of kindness and generosity are planted, one never knows what great good they will produce. This we do know: from small seeds, great deeds can grow.

THE POWER OF EMPATHY

In 1873, a Belgium Catholic Priest named Joseph Damien was sent to the Hawaiian island of Molokai to care for lepers. He arrived in high spirits, hoping to build a friendship with each of the lepers. People shunned him, however, at every turn. He built a chapel, began worship services, poured his heart out to the lepers, but all seemed futile.

No one responded to his ministry, and after twelve years of struggling, Father Damien decided to leave. As he stood in dejection on the dock waiting to board the ship, he looked down at his hands. He noticed white spots on them. Feeling some numbness, he knew immediately what was happening. He had contracted leprosy. Suddenly, he felt an empathy he had not previously known.

Father Damien returned to the leper colony and to his work. Word spread quickly and within hours, hundreds gathered outside his hut, fully identifying with his plight. A bigger surprise came the following Sunday. When he arrived at the chapel, he found it full. Father Damien began to preach from the empathy of love rather than the distance of theology, and his ministry became enormously successful.

Father Damien soon realized the power of "walking in another's shoes." Theory can be helpful, but a common experience provides a human connection.

WORDS MATTER

One day an altar boy was serving with the priest at a Sunday Mass. The Mass was in the church of the boy's rural village. The boy, nervous in his new role at the altar, accidentally dropped the wine. The priest immediately struck the boy sharply across the face. In a harsh voice, accompanied by a dismissive snarl, the priest shouted so all could hear: "Leave the altar and don't come back." That boy did exactly as the priest instructed him to do. He never came back to church again. He did become the Communist dictator of Yugoslavia. His name was Tito.

Half way around the world, in a large city cathedral, a young boy was serving a bishop at a Sunday Mass. He too accidentally dropped the wine. The bishop turned to him, but rather than responding in anger, he gently whispered with a warm twinkle in his eye, "Someday, you will likely be a priest." The boy grew up to become Archbishop Fulton Sheen, the most famous spiritual leader (and among the first to use the new medium of television) of the 1940s and 1950s.

Words have power. The childhood phrase "sticks and stones may break my bones, but words can never hurt me" simply is not true. Words can hurt, they wound and sometimes they wound deeply. But words can also reward, build, create friendships, give hope, guide, and render a blessing. Words can heal and inspire accomplishment. Words do matter.

THE TENTH BALL

Once upon a time there was a woman named June. June was the widow of a successful entrepreneur. Over a period of twenty-six years her late husband, Walter, had built a family-owned corner drugstore into a chain of fifty-eight stores with annual sales in excess of 326 million dollars.

June and Walter were the parents of a single child, Michael. Michael was a high school sophomore when his father died unexpectedly. As Michael grew toward adulthood and completed college, his mother assumed (though she never discussed it with him) that Michael would follow in his father's footsteps. It was June's expectation that Michael would run Double Discount Drugs. As president and CEO, Michael would fulfill his father's vision of one hundred stores with annual sales of over four hundred million dollars. This, June believed, was the only course her son's life could take.

June was to be disappointed. When Michael completed undergraduate school, he announced he would not be entering the family business. Greatly distraught, June sought the advice of an old family friend and confidante. In a matter of minutes, she poured out her disappointment. The old friend, who happened to be a retired high school principal, listened patiently as June wandered through various stages of grief—denial, anger, depression, and back to anger. June's pain was not new to the former principal. He had witnessed this frustration in other parents. Knowing June's disappointment was genuine, he agreed to talk with Michael.

Michael arrived early for their appointment. Rather than being reluctant to talk, Michael jumped right into the reasons for his decision.

Michael explained, "There was a time when I would have loved nothing more than to run my father's business. As a boy, I idealized my dad. I wanted to please him. I wanted to hear him say he was proud of me. But you need to understand the relationship. My father was a driven man who came up the hard way. He was determined to teach me self-reliance, but his method was demoralizing. He thought the best way to teach me self-reliance was to never encourage or praise me. He wanted me to be tough and independent."

"Two or three times a week, we played catch. Sometimes we would play catch with a baseball, at other times with a football. Either way, the goal was always the same. I was to catch the ball ten times straight. I would catch that ball eight or nine times, but always on the tenth, he would do anything to make me miss. He would throw it on the ground or over my head, but always so I had little chance of catching it." Michael paused for a long moment and then finished, "He never let me catch the tenth ball—never! No matter how hard I tried, he always set me up to fail. And I guess that's why I have to get away from my father's business; I want to catch the tenth ball."

NO EASY DEGREE

In the 1960's, Dave Bing was the NBA's leading scorer in his second year with the Detroit Pistons. Today, he is still considered one of basketball's greatest players. Bing's story did not end or begin with the Pistons. Before he went pro, he attended Syracuse University. His advisors suggested he skip the serious courses and earn an "easy" degree. After all, that is what many college athletes of his era did. Those who chose the easy academic path assumed they would always be able to rely on their athletic ability to be successful. Why add more work to the already hard work of becoming a great athlete?

Bing turned down the easy path. He took tough business classes. Bing spent hours talking with his best professors. And, he read widely, well beyond his degree focus. During his pro years, he continued his education, reading voraciously on road trips, and taking off-season jobs at a bank, in a steel mill, and the Chrysler Corporation. He picked the brain of everyone he met. His friends began to refer to him as "Mr. Interview." Today, Dave Bing is the CEO of a multi-million-dollar company that employs more than three hundred people. Bing is arguably one of the most successful black businessmen in America.

HARD WORK

Juan grew up on a Puerto Rican sugar cane plantation, the son of a farmer. He lived with his family of eight in a three-room shack with a dirt floor and no toilet. His first job, at the age of six, was to drive oxen to plow cane fields eight hours a day with no breaks; he only earned one dollar. It was in the cane fields that he learned to be on time, work hard, and be loyal and respectful of his employers. At age seven, he got a job at a golf course spotting balls for golfers.

It was there Juan began to dream of playing golf. He made a club out of a guava limb and a piece of pipe. He then hammered an empty tin can into a "ball." Next, he dug two small holes in the ground and hit the ball back and forth between them. He practiced golf with the same intensity he had put into his job in the cane field. But now, he was driving golf balls with a club, rather than oxen with a stick.

Over time, his hard work paid off. He became an excellent golfer. In time, he became a world-famous professional golfer. Over his thirty-one years on the pro circuit, Juan "Chi Chi" Rodriguez won twenty-four tournaments and earned four million dollars—nearly ten million in 2017 dollars.

Chi Chi once offered the following advice to the youth of his home village: "No matter how or where you start out in life, you can use your circumstances for your benefit. If you keep the right attitude and work hard, you can find a way to be successful." You may not achieve the kind of success that earns four million dollars, but certainly the kind of success that brings personal satisfaction and happiness.

THE MISSING SHOVEL

In *A Miracle on the River Kwai*, Ernest Gordon tells how Scottish soldiers were forced by their captors to work on a jungle railroad. They worked in deplorable conditions under barbarous guards. One day, the officer in charge became enraged over a missing shovel. He pulled his gun and promised to kill all the men unless the guilty party stepped forward. After several tense moments, a man finally stepped out of the line. The officer put his gun away, picked up a shovel, and beat the man to death in front of the other prisoners. They were allowed only to pick up his corpse and carry it with them to a second tool check. There, the tools were recounted and all the shovels were accounted for. There had never been a missing shovel. There had simply been a miscount at the first checkpoint.

Word of the incident quickly spread through the entire prison camp. An innocent man had been willing to die to save the others. The incident had a profound effect, binding the prisoners together in deep loyalty. It was this loyalty, at least in part, which gave the men the strength to survive until they were liberated. Earnest Gordon concludes his powerful narrative with these words: "No greater love has any man than that he gives his life for a friend"—certainly not original to Gordon. Even so, it is an eternal truth if ever there was one.

WINNING

Winning is a wonderful thing. It can be helpful to a career and often leads to success. Even so, it is how we handle good fortune that counts in the long run. That is what the journalist, Ellen Singer, learned in a move to avoid working a night shift.

Her newspaper editor gave her what was, for her, a nightmare assignment—a month of working the night shift. By nature a "day person," she first tried to argue her way out of the assignment rationally. It did not work. Desperate, she then tried to turn her knowledge of entertainment trivia to her advantage. Singer bet her editor that if he could beat her at a trivia contest, she would work not one but six months on the night shift. On the other hand, if she won, she would be exempt from night work for a year. In addition, she would be allotted a month of writing about anything she wanted to.

The trivia topic turned out to be the television series, *Bewitched,* and Singer easily won. Now came the bigger challenge: She had to deal with the tricky situation of having beaten her boss. To begin with, Singer used her month-at-liberty to write excellent articles which won praise for her and the paper. Instead of gloating over her victory, she told everyone who would listen that her editor had let her win on purpose in order to inspire her. The editor was understandably delighted to be given some credit for a positive outcome; also he did not forget the gracious manner in which Singer had behaved following her "win."

Singer herself should receive credit for choosing an effective career strategy. She wisely passed up the short-term prize of gloating. She invested her "win" in a long-term professional relationship which continues to create "wins" for her and for others.

ASK QUESTIONS

Asking questions is almost always a good idea. Maestro Roger Nierenberg learned this during his tenure as the conductor of the Stamford Symphony in Connecticut. He was once the guest conductor for another orchestra for which there was only one run-through of the music before the performance. When the rehearsal did not go well, Nierenberg braced himself for what he thought would be a disaster. However, on the night of the performance the orchestra's execution was perfect. What changed?

Nierenberg learned the musicians had been given almost illegible copies of the score. They struggled with the material but were able to figure things out by the time of the performance. Nierenberg realized that if he had asked questions or addressed the problem during the rehearsal, he would have discovered the problem. And, he would have been able to correct the problem in a timely manner. By saying nothing, everyone experienced more stress than was necessary.

The story serves as a good reminder of the value of asking questions—as opposed to making assumptions—when things are not working out. Taking the time to uncover a "disconnect" between the leader and the team is rarely a waste of time. It usually saves everyone a great deal of frustration.

THE OTHER WES MOORE

Meet Wes Moore. Wes Moore is a prototype when it comes to expectations found, or missing, in an environment. Moore, an African American, was three when his father died. He was raised in a minority neighborhood in Baltimore by a single mother. As an adolescent, he was a bright, but indifferent, student. He had far more interest in scoring points on the basketball court than on a biology test.

As a consequence, when he was in the eighth grade, his mother arranged to send him to a military academy. In the first month, he rebelled against the discipline and tried repeatedly to run away. But his mother kept sending him back with the same declaration: "I expect your life to matter. And, I am going to keep sending you back until you decide your life matters!"

Slowly, often with great effort, Moore learned something about himself. He liked living in an environment where he was expected to excel! He liked being a leader. In time, he became the proud leader of his squadron. This pride began to show up in the classroom. He began making his mark in academics as well as on the parade ground, football field, and basketball court.

As graduation approached, it did not occur to Moore that he might be a candidate for a Baltimore school he knew little about: Johns Hopkins University. "No one in my old neighborhood thought about going to Johns Hopkins University," he said. "We all thought we were going to the NBA."

Moore's military school record was so impressive he made it to Johns Hopkins, and there the new expectations for his life carried him even higher. He became the school's first African American Rhodes Scholar and then an officer in the elite U.S. Army Rangers. He served in Afghanistan where he received a commendation for "heroism above and beyond the call of duty." When he returned to the United States, he became a White House fellow, working alongside Secretary of State, Condoleezza Rice, in the State Department.

It was during a trip home, while serving in the State Department, that Moore's mother told him about the other Wes Moore. Moore soon learned the other Wes Moore was a man with whom he had much in common. They were both young African American men of the same age, from the same Baltimore neighborhood, with several childhood friends in common, and had the same name: Wes Moore.

The similarities ended there. The other Wes Moore was in prison, quite possibly for the rest of his life. Raised a few blocks from the childhood home of the Rhodes Scholar, Wes Moore, the other Wes Moore's life had been defined by the perils of the drug trade: a violent, lucrative, and lawless subculture. Eventually, he was involved in a robbery in which a police officer was killed. As a consequence, the other Wes Moore was sentenced to prison.

The Johns Hopkins' Rhodes Scholar, Army Ranger, and White House Fellow, Wes Moore, decided he wanted to know more about the *other Wes Moore*. He went to visit the man with whom he shared a name. Moore and the felon, Wes Moore, would have more than a dozen conversations in the year that followed. Together, they explored the *why*. Why did one find such a rewarding life and the other end up in a federal penitentiary? Moore asked the inmate if he thought the environment in which he grew up was the cause of his fate. The other Wes Moore replied: "No, it was expectations. No one expected anything of me. No one expected me to be a good student. No one cared what time I came home at night. No one cared when or if I ate. No one expected me to obey the law. No one expected my life to matter. I guess you could say, 'I met expectations.'"

VALUING PEOPLE

The Queen of England often visits Balmoral Castle. On one occasion, when she was walking by herself, it started to rain. She rushed to the shelter of the nearest cottage. A lady came to the door and was annoyed someone would bother her at that time of the morning. She opened the door a few inches and barked, "What do you want?"

The Queen did not introduce herself, she merely asked, "May I borrow an umbrella?"

"Just a minute," grumbled the woman. She slammed the door, was gone for a moment, and returned bringing the rattiest umbrella she could find, one with broken ribs and small holes. "Here."

The Queen of England thanked her and went on her way with the ragged umbrella.

The next morning, the Queen's escort, dressed in full uniform, pulled up in front of the cottage. One of the escorts knocked on the door and returned the umbrella to the woman saying, "Madam, the Queen of England thanks you."

As he walked away, he heard her mutter, "If I had only known, I'd have given her my best."

COURAGE

It was a few weeks before Christmas 1917. The beautiful snowy landscapes of Europe were blackened by war. The trenches on one side held the Germans. On the other side, the trenches were filled with Americans. It was World War I. The exchange of gunshots was intense.

Separating them was a very narrow strip of "no man's land." A young German soldier, attempting to cross that no man's land, had been shot and had become entangled in the barbed wire. He cried out in anguish, and then in pain; he continued to plead for help. Between the shells, all the Americans in that sector could hear him scream. When one American soldier could stand it no longer, he crawled out of the American trenches and, on his stomach, crawled to the German soldier. When the Americans realized what he was doing, they stopped firing, but the Germans continued. Then a German officer realized what the young American was doing and he ordered his men to cease firing as well.

Now there was a weird silence across the no man's land. On his stomach, the American made his way to the German soldier and disentangled him. He stood up with the German in his arms, walked straight to the German trenches, and placed him in the waiting arms of his comrades. Having done so, he turned and started back to the American trenches. Suddenly, there was a hand on his shoulder that spun him around. There stood a German officer who had won the Iron Cross, the highest German citation for bravery. He jerked it from his own uniform and placed it in the hand of the American who walked back to his trenches.

SPECIAL ORDERS

Horror gripped the heart of the World War I soldier as he saw his lifelong friend fall in battle. Caught in a trench with continuous gunfire whizzing over his head, the soldier asked his lieutenant if he could go out into the "no man's land" between the trenches to bring his fallen comrade back. "You can go," said the lieutenant, "but I don't think it will be worth it. Your friend is probably dead and you may throw your own life away."

The lieutenant's words did not matter and the soldier went anyway. Miraculously, he managed to reach his friend, hoist him onto his shoulder, and bring him back to their company's trench. As the two of them tumbled in together to the bottom of the trench, the officer checked the wounded soldier, then looked kindly at his friend. "I told you it wouldn't be worth it," he said, "your friend is dead, and you are now wounded."

"It was worth it, sir," the soldier insisted.

"What do you mean, it was worth it?" the lieutenant challenged, "Your friend is dead."

"Yes sir," the private answered, "but it was worth it because when I got to him, he was still alive and I had the satisfaction of hearing him say, 'Jim, I knew you'd come.'"

FINDING HOPE
THROUGH HUMOR

President Ronald Reagan's popularity in the polls rose and fell like a roller coaster. Shortly after an attempt was made to assassinate him, his ratings soared to nearly ninety percent, the highest on record. But one year later when the U. S. economy was still mired in recession, his approval ratings had plummeted to a low of thirty percent. Every other week, Dick Wirthlin, the president's pollster, reported the ratings to the president. He now had the unhappy task of telling Reagan the disturbing news.

"How are they? What do the figures look like?" Reagan asked.

"They are pretty bad, Mr. President."

"How bad are they?"

"Well, they are as low as they can get," Wirthlin answered.

"So, what do you mean?" pressed the president.

"Well, they are about thirty-two percent."

"Anything lower than that in the second year of the presidency?" Reagan asked.

"I think that's the lowest," Wirthlin replied.

Just then Reagan's face brightened and he smiled. "Dick, don't worry. I'll just go out there and try to get shot again."

This was vintage Reagan. His sense of humor was ever present. Always self-effacing, it expressed the confidence of a man who took his ideas seriously, but never himself.

ALWAYS COMPLAINING

A young woman entered a convent to prepare herself for a life of celibacy and service. The institution was one of very strict order. In addition to other regulations, the convent enforced a requirement of silence; not a word was to be uttered. Mother Superior explained to the new recruits that this rule of silence was rigid. However, once every five years, just two words could be spoken.

At the end of the first five years of service, the young novice was called in and instructed she had earned the privilege of expressing two words. What would they be? Her answer, "Food rotten."

Five years later, she was again afforded the rare privilege of speaking two more words. What would she say this time? "Beds hard."

The third time she was summoned, the woman proclaimed in exasperation, "I quit."

"Good riddance," responded Mother Superior. "All you have done since you've been here is complain."

TWO NICKELS AND FIVE PENNIES

In the days when an ice cream sundae cost much less, a ten-year-old boy entered a hotel coffee shop and sat at a table. A waitress put a glass of water in front of him. "How much is an ice cream sundae?" he asked.

"Fifty cents," replied the waitress.

The little boy pulled his hand out of his pocket and studied the coins his hand contained. "How much is a dish of plain ice cream?" he inquired.

Some people were now waiting for a table and the waitress was a bit impatient. "Thirty-five cents," she replied brusquely.

The little boy again counted the coins. "I'll have the plain ice cream," he said.

The waitress brought the ice cream, put the bill on the table, and walked away. The boy finished the ice cream, paid the cashier, and departed.

When the waitress came back, she began wiping down the table. She swallowed hard at what she saw. There, placed neatly beside the empty dish, were two nickels and five pennies: her tip.

A BOY NAMED SPARKY

There was once a boy named Sparky. For Sparky, school was all but impossible. He failed every subject in the eighth grade. He flunked physics in high school, earning a grade of zero. Sparky also flunked Latin, Algebra, and English. He did not do much better in sports. Although he did manage to make the school's golf team, he promptly lost the only important match of the season. There was a consolation match; he lost that as well.

Throughout his youth, Sparky was socially awkward. He was not actually disliked by the other students; no one cared that much. He was astonished if a classmate ever said hello to him outside of school hours. There is no way to tell how he might have done with dating. Sparky never once asked a girl to go out in high school. He was too afraid of being turned down. Sparky felt like a loser. He, his classmates ... everyone knew it, so he rolled with it. Sparky had made up his mind early in life that if things were meant to work out, they would. Otherwise, he would content himself with what appeared to be his inevitable mediocrity.

However, one thing was important to Sparky—drawing. He was proud of his artwork. Of course, no one else appreciated it. In his senior year of high school, he submitted some cartoons to the editors of the yearbook. The cartoons were rejected. Despite this rejection, Sparky was so convinced of his ability that he decided to become a professional artist.

After completing high school, he wrote a letter to Walt Disney Studios. He was told to send some samples of his artwork, and the subject for a cartoon was suggested. Sparky drew the proposed cartoon. He spent a great deal of time on it and on all the other drawings he submitted. Finally, the reply came from Disney Studios. He had been rejected once again.

So Sparky decided to write his own autobiography in cartoons. He described his childhood self, a little boy who was a chronic underachiever. This cartoon character would soon become famous worldwide. Sparky, the boy who had such a lack of success in school and whose work was rejected again and again, was Charles Schulz. He created the *Peanuts* comic strip. It was all about a little cartoon character whose kite would never fly and who never succeeded in kicking a football: Charlie Brown.

COMPASSION IS IN THE EYES

It was a bitter cold evening in northern Virginia many years ago. The old man's beard was glazed by winter's frost while he waited for a ride across the river. The wait seemed endless. His body became numb and still from the frigid north wind.

He heard the faint, steady rhythm of approaching hooves galloping along the frozen path. Anxiously, he watched as several horsemen rounded the bend. He let the first one pass by without an effort to get his attention. Then another passed by, and another. Finally, the last rider neared the spot where the old man sat like a snow statue. As this one drew near, the old man caught the rider's eye and said, "Sir, would you mind giving an old man a ride to the other side? There doesn't appear to be a passageway by foot."

Reining his horse, the rider replied, "Of course, hop aboard." Seeing the old man was unable to lift his half-frozen body from the ground, the horseman dismounted and helped the old man onto the horse. The horseman took the old man not just across the river, but to his destination, which was several miles away.

As they neared the tiny but cozy cottage, the horseman's curiosity caused him to ask, "Sir, I noticed you let several other riders pass by without making an effort to secure a ride. Then I came up and you immediately asked me for a ride. I'm curious why, on such a bitter winter night, you would wait and ask the last rider. What if I had refused and left you there?"

The old man lowered himself slowly down from the horse, looked the rider straight in the eyes, and replied, "I've been around these parts for some time. I reckon I know people pretty good." The old-timer continued, "I looked into the eyes of the other riders and immediately saw there was no concern for my situation. It would have been useless even to ask them for a ride. But when I looked into your eyes, kindness and compassion were evident. I knew, then and there, that you would welcome the opportunity to give me assistance in my time of need."

The heartwarming praise touched the horseman deeply. "I'm most grateful for what you have said," he told the old man. "May I never get too busy in my own affairs that I fail to respond to the needs of others with kindness and compassion."

With that, Thomas Jefferson turned his horse around and made his way back to the White House.

THE LUCK OF ROARING CAMP

Roaring Camp was the meanest, loudest, orneriest mining camp in all the Nevada territory. It was a place where men worked hard and played even harder. But something happened in Roaring Camp one winter night no one could have anticipated or predicted. Late on a winter's night, a child was born to Cherokee Sal, the only woman in the camp. The bad news is that in giving birth, Cherokee Sal died. The good news is the child, a baby girl, was perfectly healthy. So the men, thirty-seven in number, set about doing what they could to care for the baby.

None of the men had cared for a baby before, so they took an old apple crate and some dirty rags and laid the baby in the apple crate. It did not look quite right to them, so they drew lots and sent one of their number across the mountain to San Francisco to buy a new cherry cradle. He returned and they took the baby out of the apple crate and placed the baby in the cherry cradle with new white linens. And then they looked around the cabin and said to themselves, "This place is filthy. It is not clean enough for a baby." So they got busy and worked hard and scrubbed and cleaned the cabin until it was spotless. They even fashioned some curtains out of old flour bags. Looking at the job they had done, they were very satisfied that they had provided a clean environment for the baby.

At the end of every day as they came out of the mine, they would stand in line outside the cabin waiting to take turns holding the baby. But it was their routine not to take a bath but once a week, and they decided that holding the baby while wearing dirty clothes and having dirty hands was not good. So they passed a rule by consensus, no one could hold or play with the baby until they had cleaned up. So it was not long until the general store sold out of soap for washing men and for washing clothes.

After the men got cleaned up each day and took a turn with the baby, those who were not on duty to provide care went back to their usual practice. They would cuss and fight and drink until late in the night. But they decided that the cussing and fighting and drinking were disturbing the baby. So they passed a rule by consensus, "No drinking, cussing, or fighting after seven o'clock at night."

Little by little, the temperature of Roaring Camp came down, down, down. Until in the spring of the year, they took the baby outside to get some fresh air. It was then they noticed the ground around the cabin was scarred and torn. So they got busy and hauled in topsoil, planted grass and flowers, bushes, and trees. They created a veritable "Garden of Eden" for the baby. They wanted the baby to be surrounded by beauty whenever she was outside.

The months passed. One July evening, in the middle of the week, the men were sitting outside the cabin about eight o'clock. Clean and sober, talking with civility, they aimed to be as quiet as they could so as not to disturb the baby. As they sat there, one of their numbers looked around and said, "Who would have ever imagined us clean, sober, and quiet in the middle of the evening?"

And another one said, "Yeah, it is quite amazing, isn't it?"

And a third one said, "What my grandmother said must be true."

It was one of those moments when everybody got quiet, listened intently, and leaned forward.

"What did your grandmother say?" one of them asked.

My grandmother said that if you love the right things, they will change you for the better.

SUCCESS

To laugh often and much;
to win the respect of intelligent people
and the affection of children;
to earn the appreciation of honest critics
and endure the betrayal of false friends;
to appreciate beauty;
to find the best in others;
to leave the world a bit better,
whether by a healthy child, a garden patch,
or a redeemed social condition;
to know even one life has breathed easier because you lived;
this is to have succeeded.

Attributed
Ralph Waldo Emerson
1803-1882

A BOY AND HIS DOG

One day an eight-year-old boy went to the pet store with his dad to buy a puppy. The store manager directed them to a pen with five little furry balls huddled together. After a while, the boy noticed one of the litter all by himself in an adjacent pen. The boy asked, "Why is that puppy all alone?"

The store manager replied, "That puppy was born with a bad leg and will be crippled for life, so we're going to have to put him to sleep, we'd never be able to sell him."

"You're going to kill this puppy," the boy said sadly while patting it.

"You have to realize," said the store manager, "this puppy would never be able to run and play with a boy like you."

After a short conversation with his son, the dad told the manager they wanted to buy the puppy with the bad leg. "For the same amount of money, you could have one of the healthy ones. Why do you want this one?" the owner asked.

To answer the manager's question, the boy bent over and pulled up the pants on his right leg, exposing the brace underneath. Then the boy said, "Mister, I want this one because I understand what he is going through."

YIELD

While driving down a country road, a man came to a narrow bridge. In front of the bridge was a sign—it read, "Yield." Seeing no oncoming cars, the man continued across the bridge and onto his destination. On his way back along this same route, the man came to the same one-lane bridge from the opposite direction. To his surprise, he saw another "Yield" sign posted there. Curious, he thought, I'm sure there was a sign posted on the other side. Sure enough, when he reached the other side of the bridge and looked back, he saw the sign. Yield signs had been placed at both ends of the bridge so the drivers from both directions would give each other the right-of-way. It appeared to be a reasonable way to prevent a head-on collision.

It occurred to the man "yield" is good advice for more than the roadway. He recorded these words in his journal: *Give away everything you can and nothing you can't. Most of all, be generous when generosity costs nothing.*

JACQUELINE GAVAGAN

If good lives were built on good fortune, Jacqueline Gavagan would have reason to despair. All was well when she got out of bed September 11, 2001. She had a loving husband and a satisfying profession as a speech pathologist. Her two young children were thriving and a third was due in seven weeks. You can guess the rest. Jacqueline's husband, thirty-five-year-old Don, worked as a bond broker in the World Trade Center. By mid-morning, he was entombed in a million tons of burning rubble. So were many of the couple's closest friends.

Does she still grieve? Of course. But over the years, the Brooklynite has managed to restore meaning and even some joy to her life. She started the effort at her husband's memorial service by asking people to contribute to the fund that might save a child's life in his memory. Surgeons at NYU Medical Center had successfully repaired her own toddler's defective heart and Gavagan wanted to sponsor the operation for a child whose family could not afford it. The money flowed and soon she was back at NYU comforting a woman from Kosovo while her infant son had the surgery Jacqueline had sponsored. When asked who had fixed the boy's heart, Gavagan's beaming three-year-old answered, "Everyone who loved daddy."

THE MOST IMPORTANT TRIP

It has been accurately said that it is easy to be an angel when nobody ruffles your feathers, but it seems that "feather rufflers" will always be around.

The nineteenth century German Prince, Otto Von Bismarck, once became so incensed at the criticism of a professor that he challenged the man to a duel. Protocol dictated the one challenged was to have the choice of weapons. The professor made his choice—sausages. That is right. He sent word to Bismarck, along with a pair of sausages, that one sausage was safe to eat, the other had been poisoned with trichinae, which would cause a slow and lingering death. He informed the prince that he should choose which sausage to eat and said he would eat the other one. Bismarck reasoned that a man might die with some sort of honor on a dueling field, but never by food poisoning. He sent the message back, "His highness has destroyed the sausages and asked that you be his guest at dinner this evening. After due consideration, he feels he may have been slightly in error, and he believes an agreement can be reached."

Bismarck had concluded: "The most important trip a person ever takes is to meet someone half way."

THE EFFICIENCY EXPERT

An efficiency expert once concluded his lecture with the comment, "Please don't try these techniques at home."

"Why not?" he was asked.

"I used to watch my wife prepare breakfast and wondered why she made so many trips to the table carrying only one item at a time," he replied. "One day I asked her, 'Wouldn't it be quicker and more efficient if you organized yourself to carry several things to the table at once?'"

"Did it work?" he was asked.

"Oh yes, it worked," the expert replied. "It used to take my wife twenty minutes to prepare breakfast, now I do it in seven."

THE THIRD PEACOCK
ON THE RIGHT

Once upon a time there was a princess who was under a curse. She was asleep and no one could wake her. The only way to break the curse was with an apple from the tree that grew in the middle of the garden at the western end of the world. What does the king do? Well, on the theory that a well-run, no-risk operation makes the best of all possible worlds, the king gets out his maps, briefs his generals, and sends a couple of well-supplied divisions to the garden to fetch the apple.

The whole thing is just a matter of getting an odd prescription from an inconveniently located drugstore that doesn't deliver. In this case, the king uses his power, and the job is done. The apple is brought to the palace and applied to the princess. She wakes up; eats breakfast, lunch, and dinner forever after; and dies in bed at the respectable age of ninety-two.

Everyone knows, of course, that this is not the way to tell a good fairy tale. The story is too predictable. There's no magic. There's no *hero!* To begin with, the garden isn't on any of the maps. Only one man in the kingdom, the hundred-year-old Grand Geezer, knows where it is. When he is summoned, however, he asks to be excused. It seems he is scheduled to dine with *Beyoncé* later that evening and, therefore, cannot make the trip. He happens to have a map, but there is a complication (Isn't there always? If it's not one thing, it's another.) The map has been drawn with magical ink and will be visible only to the right man for the job. The king, of course, inquires how this man is to be found.

"Very simply," responds the Grand Geezer. "He will be recognizable by his ability to pat his head and rub his tummy at the same time, while whistling 'Puff the Magic Dragon.'"

The king calls in his nobles, all of whom are excellent musicians. They whistle, sing, and chant (Gregorian) at the paper, but nothing appears. They do their darnedest but have no luck. At last the king, in frustration, tells them to knock off for lunch and come back at two o'clock. Much too preoccupied to eat, the king strolls out onto the balcony and, lo and behold, what does he hear? Someone is walking down the road whistling "Puff the Magic Dragon" while patting the top of his head and rubbing his stomach all at the same time.

It is, of course, the miller's son, a local high school dropout and village rowdy. The king, however, is not one to balk at ideologies when he needs help. He hauls the boy in, gives him the map, and sends him off with a bag of bagels (sourdough) and a bottle of his best merlot.

That night the boy reads the map. It seems pretty straightforward, except for a warning at the bottom in block capitals: **AFTER ENTERING THE GARDEN GO STRAIGHT TO THE TREE, PICK THE APPLE, AND GET OUT. DO NOT, UNDER ANY CIRCIRCUMSTANCES, SPEAK TO THE THIRD PEACOCK ON THE RIGHT.**

Any child worth his PSP (*Play Station Portable*) can write the rest of the story. The boy goes into the garden and gets as far as the third peacock on the right. The third peacock on the right startles him by asking, "Wouldn't you like a Butterfinger candy bar and a nice frosty mug of root beer?"

Exhausted and parched from his long journey, the boy gobbles the candy bar and guzzles down the root beer. Before he knows it, he has fallen fast asleep. When he wakes up, he is in a pitch-black cave; a light flickers, a voice calls—and from there on all hell breaks loose. The boy follows an invisible guide with a cocked hat down rivers of fire in an aluminum dinghy. He is imprisoned by the Crown Prince of the Salamanders. Finally, he is rescued by a confused eagle (who looks a lot like Jim Carey) who deposits him at the eastern end of the world.

In the dead of the winter, the boy works his way back to the western end of the world. He gets the apple (having learned through trial and error not to speak to the third peacock on the right), brings it to the castle, and touches it to the princess' lips. He awakens her, reveals himself to be the long-lost son of the Eagle King, and marries the princess. Then, and only then, do they live happily ever after.

It is the improbability and risk that make the story. There isn't a child on earth who doesn't know the crucial moment—whose heart, no matter how well he knows the story, doesn't skip a beat every time the boy comes to the third peacock on the right. There is no one in touch with his humanity who doesn't recognize that moment as an opportunity for the boy to prove that he matters despite his past mistakes. This is the second chance he's been hoping for, the chance to prove he can get it right. This is the moment that witnesses the birth of the *hero within.*

THE ANTS AND THE GRASSHOPPER

One bright day in late autumn a family of Ants were bustling about in the warm sunshine. They were busy drying the grain they had stored for the coming winter. As the Ants worked, a starving Grasshopper, his fiddle under his arm, came up and begged for a bite to eat.

"What!" cried the Ants in surprise. "Haven't you stored anything away for the winter? What in the world were you doing all summer?"

"I didn't have time to store up any food," whined the Grasshopper. "I was so busy playing my fiddle and having a good time that before I knew it the summer was gone."

The Ants shrugged their shoulders in disbelief. "Making music, were you?" they cried. "Very well, now dance! It seems to us you had the same opportunity to prepare for the winter as did we." And they turned their backs to the Grasshopper and went on with their work.

As they scrambled away, the wisest and oldest Ant counseled the others: "Let the Grasshopper be a reminder. There's a time for work and a time for play."

SNAKES AND ALLIGATORS

Once upon a time a wealthy entrepreneur bought a huge ranch in Wyoming. As soon as he was settled he invited some of his closest associates to see it. After touring the 3,500 acres of mountains and rivers and grasslands, he ushered everybody into the house. The house was as spectacular as the scenery. Out back was the largest swimming pool anyone had ever seen. However, it was not a pool in which anyone would want to swim. The pool was filled with alligators and poisonous snakes of every description.

The eccentric owner explained the pool: "I value courageous risk-taking above everything else. As far as I'm concerned, the courage to take a risk is what made me a billionaire. In fact, I think that courage is such a powerful virtue I'll make each of you the same offer. The first person who is courageous enough to dive in that pool and swim the length of it can have his choice of my house, my land, or my money." Of course, everybody had a good laugh at the rancher's robust, but absurd challenge. Everyone proceeded to follow the owner into the house for lunch.

Suddenly, the clamor of footsteps and laughter were interrupted by a splash! Turning around, the guests saw one of their members swimming for his life across the pool. He thrashed at the water as snakes and alligators swarmed after him. After several death-defying seconds, the man climbed out of the pool, unharmed, on the other side.

The host was amazed, but stuck to his promise. He said. "You are indeed a man of courage and I will stick to my word. What do you want? You can have your choice—my house, my land, my money—just name it and it's yours."

The young man looked at the host with anger and revenge in his eyes and said, "Mister, all I want is the name of the guy who pushed me into the pool."

Leadership

THE TONDELAYO

In the book, *The Fall of Fortresses*, Elmer Bendiner tells of a miracle which took place aboard the B17 bomber, the Tondelayo. During a run over Kassel, Germany, the plane was barraged by Nazi anti-aircraft guns. That in itself was not unusual, but on this particular flight, the plane's fuel tank was hit. The following morning, the pilot, Bohn Fawkes, asked the crew chief for the shell as a souvenir of their unbelievable luck. Bohn was then told that not just one shell had been found in the fuel tank, but eleven. The shells were sent to the armorers to be defused.

Later they informed the Tondelayo crew that when they opened the shells, they found no explosive charge in any of them. One of the shells, however, contained a carefully rolled piece of paper. On it was scrawled in the Czech language; "This is all we can do for you now."

The miracle had not been one of misfired shells, but of forced labor. The Czech Patriots did what little they could do for the war effort. The deed seemed small to them; it did not seem small to the Tondelayo crew.

THE CORRECT STORY

Once upon a time there was a vice president of engineering named Leo, whose company made high-quality, capital goods equipment. Having been with the company for thirty years, Leo was a good engineer who knew the product inside and out. Over the years he had come to know the customers as well. He was proud of and personally involved in the design and installation of the product. It was not unusual to see him coatless and with his tie loose, perched on a stool before a drafting board surrounded by young engineers, grappling with a tough installation problem. While some thought Leo did too much, others felt with him on the job the customer would be satisfied.

One day, however, the company became a wholly owned subsidiary when the president, whose family owned the company, sold it to a competitor. One allied product line was acquired, and then another. The organization streamlined its efforts and Leo's department was required to do the engineering for their product line and for several other subsidiaries as well.

Now Leo's job had changed, and trouble began to brew for Leo because he couldn't seem to change with the situation. Leo had always viewed himself as a one-man department (with assistants as trainees) who personally engineered the product for his friend, the customer. Initially, he resisted working on the engineering problems of sister companies whose customers and products he barely knew and cared little about. His new designation as corporate vice president of engineering seemed just another unnecessary complication. Nothing worked the way it used to. Leo saw himself bypassed through progress and change, and he did not like it.

As Leo's frustration grew, he worked even harder. His longing for the good old days forced him into an ever-faster run to know more customers and more product lines. Often working evenings, he franticly forced new systems to fit old procedures. And, of course, he began to slip. Gradually, Leo came to be viewed by his colleagues as *good old Leo*. Company leadership began to do an end run around Leo. "Let's not let Leo in on this one or he'll take it over and we'll get bogged down," was a sentiment often expressed. His direct reports considered Leo a fine fellow but a bit out of touch.

Fortunately, before the situation forced a major organizational shift, Leo took stock of his situation and saw himself as he was. His self-image of a hands-on engineer was no longer applicable to the corporation's greatly-expanded needs. Leo had been telling himself an incorrect story. Against all evidence to the contrary, he had assured himself the world had not changed. The new organization just needed time to fully understand his way of doing things. Courageously, and with no small amount of discomfort, he looked in the mirror and told himself the correct story. The world had changed. Consequently, he had better adjust to the change or he would be left behind!

At that moment, with a new perspective and the courage to face it, Leo began to change. He began focusing on how his years of experience could be applied to the coaching of his direct reports. He consciously placed himself in the role of corporate vice president of engineering. He began to understand how to better mesh gears with the new reality of the world around him. He stopped pushing back against centralized procedures and processes. Leo began the most challenging re-engineering job of his career—changing Leo. In the process, Leo gained a powerful professional insight: The more accurate one's view of self, the greater the degree of professional and personal effectiveness.

As Leo thought through this discovery, he realized what he needed to do with Leo was what he had always done with equipment and processes: Be tenaciously committed to the truth, be objective, and make reality-based decisions. He would never have engineered a piece of equipment based on what he preferred to believe; or abandoned facts in favor of feeling good. Leo chose to apply to himself the same capacity for critique which he routinely applied to engineering specs. Leo realized low self-awareness coupled with low self-critique functions like a filter. Without self-critique, self-concept screens out what each person does not want to hear and see and allows through only the information the person wants to hear and see. Utilizing his excellent problem-solving skills, Leo accurately concluded: "A person cannot (and will not) fix what is broken until they admit it is broken." Nothing changes until it becomes what it is.

MOSES

If you had seen her, your first reaction might not have been positive. She wasn't a very impressive-looking woman—just a little over five feet tall in her late thirties with dark brown weathered skin. She could not read or write. The clothes she wore were old and worn. When she smiled, people could see plainly her top two front teeth were missing. She lived alone.

Her employment was intermittent. Most of the time, she took domestic jobs in small hotels scrubbing floors, tidying up rooms, and cooking. But just about every spring and fall, she would disappear from her place of employment. A couple of weeks later she'd come back broke and work again to scrape together what money she could. When she was present on the job, she worked hard and seemed physically tough. But she was also known to have bouts where she would suddenly fall asleep—sometimes in the middle of a conversation. She attributed this affliction to a blow to the head she had taken during a teenage fight.

Who would respect a woman like that? Who could possibly respect a woman with such a history? The answer is that more than three hundred slaves followed her to freedom out of the South. They recognized and respected her leadership. So did just about every abolitionist in New England. The year was 1857; the woman's name was Harriet Tubman. While she was only in her thirties, Harriet Tubman came to be called Moses because of her ability to go into the land of captivity and bring so many of her people out of bondage.

ONE MORE ROUND

Prizefighter, James Corbett, made many memorable statements during his colorful career. Perhaps his most famous was when he was asked, "What is the most important thing for a man to do to become a champion?" Corbett replied, "Fight one more round." Many successful people have had that perspective. Thomas Gray wrote seventy-five drafts of "Eulogy Written in a Church Yard" before he was satisfied with his poetic masterpiece. S. M. Behrman, an American playwright, wrote plays for eleven years before he sold one. Somerset Maughan earned only five hundred dollars in his first ten years as a writer. While working full-time in a factory, Enrico Caruso studied voice for twelve years before he became a successful performer. George Gershwin composed almost one hundred melodies before he sold his first one for five dollars. During his first five years as a writer, Zane Grey could not sell a single story.

Determination is often the decisive factor in the realization of a dream. Behavioral scientists tell us ten thousand hours are required to master an art or craft. Pursue your craft or talent, study and learn, grow by experience, and keep working. The victory often goes to those who are willing to fight "one more round."

THE MAD MAN AND THE LAW

He was the most hated and vilified congressman of his time, a stubborn, ill-humored man who delighted in agitating his peers. During his time in office, Monday was the official petition day in the House of Representatives. On that day, any member of the House could introduce petitions for consideration. And every Monday morning, his fellow congressmen entered the chamber with a feeling of great dread. If they spotted the bulky legislator in seat 203 of the House, they knew they were in for a very long day.

It seemed he always came in with the same set jaw, the same determined look, and when he stood to speak, it was always about the same thing, "That abominable law," as he put it. At one point, it was reported that he introduced nine hundred petitions against the law in one day. One of his fellow congressmen called him a "mischievous, bad old man." And some newspapers dubbed him "The mad man of Massachusetts."

Who was this devious troublemaker? Who was this rabble-rouser who dared to speak against a law that had been legitimized by every government since 1787? He was John Quincy Adams. His courageous battle against slavery provoked some of the most explosive showdowns and outrageous maneuvers in Congressional history. His stand was all the more noteworthy because he did not have to take a stand to become famous. His reputation and his place in history were already secured. As the sixth President of the United States, he was entitled to retire to a life of reflective ease. But after his loss to Andrew Jackson in the Presidential race of 1828, his neighbors approached him in 1830 to run as their congressman. He accepted the honor and was handily elected. And so he arrived back in Washington, D.C. as a sixty-year-old freshman congressman beginning, perhaps, the greatest struggle of his political life.

As early as 1820, Adams had been engaged in the growing controversy over slavery. He had publicly spoken against it on moral grounds in debates with John C. Calhoun, all the while hoping a more articulate spokesman would take up the cause. But in the House of Representatives in 1830, a more articulate spokesman than Adams was not to be found. So, he filled this role with a tremendous sense of duty and purpose.

By 1836, some Southern congressmen had had enough. Voting 117 to 68, they passed a gag rule that tabled all decisions relating to slavery. The rule allowed no discussion whatsoever, much less referral to committee for action. Over the next eight years, continuing gag orders were adopted. And during those eight years, Adams continued to present his petition using every bit of expertise and cunning his forty years in politics provided him. He managed to get the substance of each petition into the congressional record. He did this by artfully asking if a petition stating, "Slavery should be outlawed" would be against "the rule?" His daily battle to repel the gag rules infuriated his opponents as much as his stand against slavery. He could never rise to his feet to speak without enduring a jarring round of ridicule, repeated motions of censure, and loud calls for his expulsion.

But his courage never flagged. He remained a constant irritant to the status quo, a constant prod to the slow of conscience, a constant reminder of the immorality and illogic of men owning men, and a constant voice for those he represented. Finally, in 1844, the twenty-first gag rule was repealed. Adams had won the right to continue to petition against slavery. By that time, even his enemies acknowledged his courage and integrity. They called him, "Old man eloquent." He died in 1846 after collapsing at his desk in the House, never having seen the abolition of the law he so despised.

While he accomplished many other great things in his career, John Quincy Adams' prolonged battle to abolish slavery has marked him, perhaps even more than his presidency, as a man of moral courage. He dared to speak out when it was neither comfortable nor safe to do so. He dared to speak out when his personal reputation and safety were threatened. And he continued to speak out when there seemed to be no hope that he would ever be heard. That is the essence of courage: Doing what is right simply because it is right.

RIGHTEOUS AMONG
THE NATIONS

One morning in late July of 1940, Japanese Consul General, Chiune Sugihara, awakened to find a throng of Jewish refugees outside the gate of the Japanese Consulate in Lithuania. Most of them had fled from Poland, barely escaping the grasp of the Nazis during their invasion of that country. But once again, with the Nazis advancing, they were trapped.

On that morning, they were seeking the help of Sugihara because word had spread among them that there was still one way out of Lithuania. They could travel through the Soviet Union into Japan and on to freedom in the Caribbean. The only thing they lacked was transit visas from the Japanese Government.

Sugihara, a forty-year-old diplomat with a promising career, immediately wired Tokyo to obtain permission to write the visas. His government denied his request. He wired them again, and again they refused. He tried a third time and was not only refused, but was told to stop asking. Sugihara faced a dilemma. On the one hand, he was a faithful Japanese taught from birth to respect and obey authority. If he disregarded his orders, his family would probably be disgraced and their lives would be in jeopardy. On the other hand, he was from a Samurai family, taught to help people in need. Further, he was also a Christian, having converted as a young man.

His choice was clear. For the next twenty-nine days, he and his wife, Yukiko, spent every moment writing transit visas.

Normally, a consulate might write three hundred visas in a month. Sugihara wrote more than that number each day. He did not stop to eat, instead snacking on sandwiches as he wrote, and he barely slept. On August 28, 1940, he was forced to close the consulate and depart for Tokyo. But still he refused to stop writing, even to the last second. As his train prepared to pull out of the station, he continued signing visas. When he could do no more, with his train gaining speed as it left the station, he tossed his consult visa stamp to a refugee so it could be used in his absence.

For a few more years, Sugihara managed to stay in the diplomatic corps, but was then dismissed. His days in government leadership were over. Back in Japan, he found part-time work as an interpreter. Later, his knowledge of Russian helped him land a job as a manager for an export company, and he lived in relative obscurity.

Some people lead for a lifetime, others receive only a moment to show the way. Chiune Sugihara made the most of his brief opportunity. It is estimated that more than six thousand people were saved from concentration camps as a result of his leadership, the second largest number of Jews ever rescued from the Nazis. In 1985, Sugihara was awarded Israel's highest honor, recognition as *Righteous Among the Nations.*

RICKENBACKER

What do these three men have in common: the auto racer who set the world's speed record at Daytona in 1914, the pilot who recorded the highest number of victories in aerial combat in World War I, and the secretary of war's special advisor who survived a plane crash and twenty-two days on a raft in the Pacific during World War II? They all lived through dangerous circumstances, they all displayed courage and steely nerves under duress, and they all happen to be the same person, Eddie Rickenbacker.

Meeting a challenge was never a big problem for Eddie Rickenbacker, whether it was physical, mental, or economic. When he was twelve, his father died and he quit school to become the family's primary breadwinner. He sold newspapers, eggs, and goat's milk. He worked in a glass factory, brewery, shoe factory, and foundry. Then as a teenager, he started working as a racecar mechanic, and at age twenty-two, he began racing. Two years later, he set the world speed record.

When the United States entered World War I, Rickenbacker tried to enlist as an aviator, but was over age and undereducated. So instead, he entered as a chauffeur and then talked his superiors into sending him to flight training. Despite not fitting in with his college educated fellow aviators, he excelled as a pilot. By the time the war was over, he had logged three hundred combat hours, the most of any American pilot. He survived one hundred, thirty-four aerial encounters with the enemy, claiming twenty-six kills. He earned the Medal of Honor and eight Distinguished

Service Crosses, as well as the French Legion of Honor. He was also promoted to Captain and put in command of his squadron. Rickenbacker's prowess in the air caused the press to dub him the "American Ace of Aces." When asked about his courage in combat, he confessed he had been afraid. "Courage," he said, "is doing what you're afraid to do. There can be no courage unless you're scared." That courage served the Ace of Aces well during World War I.

In 1933, he became the vice president of Eastern Air Transport, later known as Eastern Air Lines. Back then, all airlines existed only because they were subsidized by the government, but Rickenbacker thought they should be self-sufficient. He decided to completely change the way the company did business. Within two years, he made Eastern profitable, a first in aviation history. And when the President of the United States cancelled all commercial carriers' airmail contracts, Rickenbacker took him on and won. Rickenbacker led Eastern successfully for thirty years and retired at age seventy-three. When he died ten years later, his son, William, wrote, "If he had a motto, it must have been the phrase I've heard a thousand times, 'If you're gonna lead, do what's right and do it now.'"

A DISASTER OFF THE
SCILLY ISLES

In the dense fog of a dark night in October 1707, Great Britain lost nearly an entire fleet of ships. There was no pitched battle at sea. The Admiral, Clowdisley Shovell, simply miscalculated his position in the Atlantic and his flagship smashed into the rocks of the Scilly Isles, a tail of islands off the southwest coast of England. The rest of the fleet, following blindly behind, went aground and piled onto the rocks, one after the other. Four ships and two thousand lives were lost.

For such a proud nation of seafarers, this tragic loss was embarrassing. But to be fair to the memory of Clowdisley Shovell, it was not altogether surprising. The concept of latitude and longitude had been around since the first century B.C. But by 1700, we still had not managed to devise an accurate way to measure longitude. Nobody ever knew for sure how far east or west they had traveled. Professional seamen, like Clowdisley Shovell, had to estimate their progress by guessing their average speed or by dropping a log over the side of the boat and finding how long it took it to float from bow to stern. Forced to rely on such crude measurements, the Admiral can be forgiven his misjudgment.

What caused the disaster was not the Admiral's ignorance, but his inability to measure something that he already knew to be critically important, in this case, longitude. I suppose you could say the lesson of Clowdisley Shovell is caution is a virtue, even for those who have a lot of mileage and a lot of experience.

ROCK CONCERT

Even without the torn jeans, he made a scruffy looking ten-year-old. His fifth-grade classmates had never seen anyone as poorly dressed as Marco. This was his first day of elementary school in a quaint New England town of well-to-do families.

Marco's parents were migrant fruit pickers and his classmates eyed him with suspicion. Even though they whispered and made comments about his clothes, he did not seem to notice. Then came recess and the kick ball game. Marco led off the first inning with a home run, earning him a bit of respect from his wardrobe critics. Next up to kick was Richard, the least athletic and most overweight child in the class. After his second strike, amid the groans of his classmates, Marco edged up to Richard and quietly said, "Forget them kid. You can do it. Kick it."

Richard kicked a home run and at that precise moment, something began to change in Marco's class. Over the next few months, Marco was able to teach the class many new things. Things such as how to tell when fruit is ripe, how to draw a turkey, and especially how to treat other people.

By the time Marco's parents finished their work in the area, the class was preparing to celebrate Christmas. While other students brought the teacher fancy scarves, perfumes, and soaps, Marco stepped up to the teacher's desk with a special gift. It was a rock that he delivered into the teacher's hands which was beautiful and bright. "I polished it up especially for you," he said.

Years later, the teacher still had Marco's rock on her desk. At the beginning of each school year, she would tell her class about the gentle boy who taught her and her class not to judge a book by its cover. It is what is on the inside of others that truly counts.

ROSWELL MCINTYRE

During the American Civil War, a young man named Roswell McIntyre was drafted into the New York Calvary. The war was not going well, and soldiers were needed so desperately that he was sent into battle with very little training. Roswell became frightened. He panicked and ran. He was later court marshaled and condemned to be shot for desertion. McIntyre's mother appealed to President Lincoln. She pleaded that he was young and inexperienced and needed a second chance. The generals, however, urged the President to enforce discipline. Exceptions, they asserted, would undermine the discipline of an already beleaguered army.

Lincoln thought and prayed and then he wrote a famous statement, "I have observed," he said, "that it never does a boy much good to shoot him." He wrote this letter in his own handwriting, "This letter will certify that Roswell McIntyre is to be readmitted into the New York Calvary. When he serves out his required enlistment, he will be freed of any charges of desertion."

That faded letter, signed by the president, is on display in the Library of Congress and attached there is a note, which reads, "This letter was taken from the body of Roswell McIntyre, who died at the battle of Little Five Forks, Virginia."

THE ELEPHANT IN THE ROOM

Once upon a time there were six blind men. The blind men sat around a table talking about things they would like to see if, in fact, they could see. As they talked, they all agreed that one of the things they had always wanted to see was an elephant. As they came to this agreement, they heard what they believed to be the sound of an elephant outside the house where they were seated. Together, in a single file, they went out into the street and began to examine the elephant the only way blind men can examine an elephant—by touching the elephant.

One blind man took hold of the elephant's tail and said to himself, "Who would have thought it? An elephant is nothing more than a rope, just a rope."

The second touched the elephant's massive hind leg and thought to himself, "Who would have thought it? An elephant is a tree trunk, just a great big tree trunk."

The third ran his hands along the massive side of the elephant and concluded, "What a strange animal. An elephant is a wall, just a big wall."

The fourth took hold of the elephant's ear and holding the ear between his hands observed, "Hmm, quite interesting. An elephant is like a carpet, a carpet one would place on a floor."

And then the fifth man took hold of the elephant's tusk and, running his hands along the tusk thought, "This must be the most unusual animal in the world. It's a spear, just like any other spear a soldier would throw in battle."

Finally, the sixth man took hold of the elephant's trunk as

it wiggled about. He said to himself, with a bit of humor, "Who would have imagined that an elephant is nothing more than a fat snake."

Having examined the elephant, the six blind men filed back into the house and sat down around the table and began to share their observations. The first man began, "I suppose you guys are surprised to discover an elephant is just a rope–a rope one would use to tie up a bundle of sticks."

The second spoke up, "I don't know where you were, but the elephant I examined was like a tree trunk."

The third man reacted, "Both of you are wrong. The elephant is like a wall."

The fourth chimed in, "I have no idea where you guys were, but the elephant I examined was like a carpet, that's all. Just a carpet you would place on the floor."

The fifth man added, "It's hard to believe that all four of you could be so wrong. An elephant is like a spear. I suspect everyone knows that, or at least anyone who has ever touched an elephant."

Finally, the sixth man stated, "This is interesting. Apparently, there were other animals outside the house. The elephant I examined was nothing like the animal you've described. To me an elephant is just a big fat, wiggling snake."

And so they began to argue, each one in turn pushing his perspective, insisting he was right and the others were wrong. Shortly, a sighted friend came by and the blind men posed a question. "We're glad you're here, we need your help in settling a dispute. We've just examined an elephant and we want to know which one of us is right."

The first man told of his experience, "An elephant is like a rope."

The second asserted, "An elephant is a like a tree trunk."

"No," insisted the third man, "An elephant is like a massive wall."

"An elephant is like a carpet," the fourth asserted.

The fifth man proclaimed, "An elephant is like a spear."

Finally, the sixth man insisted that an elephant is "like a fat, wiggling snake."

After listening to each of the men's assertions as to what an elephant is like, the sighted friend thought for a moment and responded. "Individually, you are all wrong. Together, you are all right."

CHOICE AND CONSEQUENCE

William McKinley, the twenty-fifth President of the United States [1897 to 1901] once had to choose between two equally qualified men for a key job. He puzzled over the choice until he remembered a long-ago incident.

On a rainy night, McKinley had boarded a crowded streetcar. One of the he was considering had also been aboard, though he did not see McKinley. Then, an old woman carrying a basket of laundry struggled into the car, looking in vain for a seat. The job candidate pretended not to see her and kept his seat. McKinley gave up his seat to her. Remembering this episode, which he called, "An omission of kindness," McKinley decided not to hire the man on the street car.

DO SOMETHING GREAT

Abraham Lincoln often slipped out of the White House on Wednesday evenings to listen to the sermons of Dr. Phineas Gurley at New York Avenue Presbyterian Church. He generally preferred to come and go unnoticed. So when Dr. Gurley knew the president was coming, he left his study door open. On one of those occasions, the president quietly entered through a side door of the church, took his seat in the minister's study located just off the sanctuary, and propped the door open just wide enough to hear the preacher.

During the walk home on Wednesday evening, an aide asked President Lincoln his appraisal of the sermon. The president thoughtfully replied, "The content was excellent. He delivered it with eloquence; he had put work into the message."

"Then you thought it was an excellent sermon?" questioned the aide.

"No," Lincoln answered.

"But you said that the content was excellent, it was delivered with eloquence, and it showed much work," the aide pressed.

"That's true," Lincoln said, "But Dr. Gurley forgot the most important ingredient. He forgot to ask us to do something great—to live for something more than ourselves."

REAL MEN

Jim was fourteen years old in the summer of 1955. He was spending that summer the way he had spent so many summers at his grandfather's farm. It was a place where he could do all the things that he had heard his father and grandfather talk about. He could tramp through the woods for hours at a time, fish in the nearby fishing hole, and swim.

Jim admired his grandfather mainly because he was for him a good friend. Jim and his grandfather sat in the porch swing one Sunday afternoon. As they sat, they talked about the previous day's fishing trip. They had not been seated long when Jim's grandmother came out and announced they were ready to cut the cake celebrating Jim's cousin's birthday. She said, "You fellas get your voices ready because we're going to be singing 'Happy Birthday.'"

At this point, Jim said to his grandfather, "Granddad, real men don't sing."

With raised eyebrows his grandfather responded, "Is that so?" Jim's grandfather got up and went in the house and joined in the singing. Jim sat in the porch swing mulling over the wisdom of what he had just shared with his grandfather, "Real men don't sing."

The years would pass, some twelve years to be exact and at twenty-six years of age, Jim would receive word of his grandfather's passing. Jim made his way back to the farm and the small community church where the funeral would be.

That afternoon, after the funeral and after lunch, Jim sat in the small office his grandfather had fashioned for himself out of an old canning room in the farmhouse. And sitting there in his grandfather's chair he saw the mementos of a lifetime. He saw his grandfather's diploma as he graduated second in his class from the U. S. Naval Academy at Annapolis. He saw also his citations for bravery, three in number. And he saw a letter of thanks from President Franklin Delano Roosevelt. The president was thanking his grandfather, who at sixty-one years of age had applied for retirement when Pearl Harbor was bombed. His grandfather had withdrawn his request for retirement and served through the course of the war.

Finally, his eyes fell upon a citation issued by the President of the United States and the Secretary of the Navy. The citation stated Jim's grandfather had been the oldest officer decorated for heroism at the Battle of the Coral Sea in 1944.

As Jim sat in his grandfather's chair looking at the mementos of his long life, the words he had spoken to his grandfather so many summers before came back to him, "Granddad, real men don't sing." He remembered how his grandfather had gone in the house and sang—despite Jim's observation concerning "real men."

It was then Jim remembered something else. He remembered something his grandfather used to say to him whenever someone was hard headed or unreasonable or just plain immature. His grandfather would shake his head patiently and say, "We just have to be patient with people Jim, while they learn what we can never tell them." It was that afternoon that Jim understood what his grandfather meant.

LITTLE BY LITTLE

Anne Schreiber was one hundred and one years old when she died in January of 1995. For years, she had lived in a tiny, rundown, rent-controlled studio apartment in Manhattan. The paint on the walls was peeling and the old bookcases that lined the walls were covered in dust. Rent was four hundred dollars a month. Schreiber lived on Social Security and a small monthly pension, which she started receiving in 1943 when she retired as an auditor for the Internal Revenue Service. She had not done very well at the IRS. More specifically, the agency had not done very well by her. Despite having a law degree and doing excellent work, she was never promoted and when she retired at age fifty-one, she was earning only $3,150 a year.

Schreiber was the very model of thrift. She did not spend money on herself. She did not buy new furniture as the old pieces wore out. She did not even subscribe to a newspaper. About once a week, she would go to the public library and read the Wall Street Journal.

Imagine the surprise of Norman Lamm, the president of Yeshiva University in New York when he found out that Anne Schreiber, who he had never heard of and who had never attended Yeshiva, left nearly her entire estate to the University. "When I saw the will, it was mind-blowing. Such an unexpected windfall," said President Lamm. This woman has become a legend overnight.

Anne Schreiber left Yeshiva University twenty-two million dollars. Shortly before her death, Anne told her rabbi, "I've tried to live carefully. I want to leave something behind."

THE WINE BARREL

Once upon a time, there was a village, which enjoyed great prosperity. Every family had all that it needed and more.

At the heart of the community's prosperity was the generosity of the king. You see, the king owned the village lock, stock, and barrel. And indeed, barrels came in handy inasmuch as the village economy was based on the wine it produced.

Surrounding the village were acre after acre of the most fertile soil anyone could have hoped for. Every village family had ample acreage for the growing of large, luscious grapes. And when the grapes were harvested, every family had full access to the winepresses, bottles, and corks. With only modest effort, a family could do quite well.

In exchange for the use of the fields and the winery, the king asked each family to give him ten percent of the wine they produced each year. Everyone felt this was a most generous gesture on the part of the king. And so, every fall, each family gladly delivered to the king ten of every one hundred barrels of wine they produced.

Things went well for many years. Then came a year when the weather was disagreeable. As a result, the harvest was the poorest in memory. And, to everyone's disappointment, the following year was even worse.

Feeling concern for the difficulties the villagers were facing, the king came to them with a proposal. "For this year, forget about the ten percent agreement. Instead, I would like for each of you to simply pay me what you can. In fact, I am going to place a single barrel in the village square. I will leave it there for one week. During the week, I would like for each family to place in the barrel whatever amount of wine they can afford. I will consider myself paid in full with the contents of this single barrel."

Over the following week, each family made their way to the barrel, lifted the lid, and contributed something.

At the end of the week, the king came with his wagon and collected the barrel. As the king's wagon towed the barrel up the hill to the castle, the king could tell it was brimming over. He thought to himself, "I imagine they have all given me a portion of their best wine. After all, I have asked so little of them this year."

Reaching the castle, the king hurried to dip his royal cup into the barrel. Closing his eyes and savoring the anticipated taste of the wine, he drank deeply, holding the cup with both hands. It was then that his heart sank as he realized his cup was filled with nothing but water.

THE BROOKLYN BRIDGE

The Brooklyn Bridge which spans the river between Manhattan and Brooklyn is an engineering wonder. In 1883, a creative engineer, John Roebling, was inspired by an idea for this spectacular bridge project. However, bridge-building experts told him to forget it, it was just not possible. Roebling convinced his son, Washington, an up-and-coming engineer, the bridge could be built. The two of them conceived the idea of how it could be accomplished and how to overcome the obstacles. Somehow, they convinced bankers to finance the project. Then, with excitement and energy, they hired their crew and began to build their dream bridge.

The project had been under way for only a few months when a tragic on-site accident killed John Roebling and severely injured his son. Washington was severely damaged, unable to talk or walk. Everyone thought the project would have to be scrapped. The Roeblings were the only ones who understood how the bridge could be built.

Though Washington Roebling was unable to move or talk, his mind was as sharp as ever. One day as he lay in his hospital bed, an idea flashed in his mind as to how to develop a communication code. All he could move was one finger, so he touched the arm of his wife with that finger. He tapped out a code with which to communicate to her. She, in turn, was to tell the engineers who continued building the bridge. For thirteen years, Washington tapped out his instructions with one finger until the spectacular Brooklyn Bridge was finally completed.

AN ACT OF KINDNESS

During the Civil War President Abraham Lincoln often visited hospitals where he would talk with wounded soldiers. Doctors pointed to a young soldier who was near death. Lincoln went over to his bedside.

"Is there anything I can do for you?" asked the President.

The soldier obviously did not recognize Lincoln, and with some effort he was able to whisper, "Would you please write a letter to my mother?"

A pen and paper were provided and the President carefully began writing down what the young man was able to say:

"My dearest mother, I was badly hurt while doing my duty. I'm afraid I'm not going to recover. Don't grieve too much for me, please. Kiss Mary and John for me. May God bless you and father."

The soldier was too weak to continue, so Lincoln signed the letter for him and added, "Written for your son by Abraham Lincoln."

The young man asked to see the note and was astonished when he discovered who had written it. "Are you really the President?" he asked.

"Yes, I am," Lincoln replied quietly. Then he asked if there was anything else he could do.

"Would you please hold my hand?" the soldier asked. "It will help to see me through to the end."

In the hushed room, the tall gaunt President took the boy's hand in his and waited quietly until death came.

NO TIME TO HESITATE

In 1972, Jacob, a twenty-four-year-old Chicago firefighter, made a lightning-fast decision that would save two lives. The first life was that of Chris, a seven-year-old boy. As Jacob evacuated trapped residents from a burning building, he sensed someone was still inside. Then a young mother screamed, "Where is my Chris?"

Against his better judgment, Jacob returned to the inferno. He fought his way through a flaming hallway to pull the boy to safety. But that was just the start of their story.

Over the next twenty years, Jacob and Chris became fast friends. Jacob provided the guidance and love the fatherless Chris needed. Every week, Chris visited Jacob at the firehouse.

The second life Jacob saved? His own. In the early 1990s, Jacob was struck with diabetes and needed a new kidney. When Chris found out, he hesitated no longer than Jacob had that critical moment years before: "I've got two kidneys and you can have one." Little did Jacob know, all those years before, in saving Chris, he had saved himself.

THE COMMON GOOD

President Abraham Lincoln once remarked, "Nearly all men can stand adversity, but if you want to test a man's character, give him power." Few people have more power than an American President. Being the leader of the free world can certainly go to a person's head, but not to Jimmy Carter's. If you review his career from the time he was a school board official to his term in the White House and beyond, you can see that he was willing to take on nearly any role to achieve a goal he believed in. He always embraced the importance of the common good.

There is possibly no more vivid example of his belief in the importance of the common good than his work with Habitat for Humanity. Habitat was officially founded by Millard and Linda Fuller in 1976. The goal of the organization is big: to eliminate poverty level housing and homelessness from the world. In the late 70s and early 80s, they began their bold venture. After six years, they had built houses internationally in Mexico, Zaire, and Guatemala. And in the United States, they had affiliates building houses in San Antonio, Texas; Americus, Georgia; Johns Island, South Carolina; and other locations in Florida and Appalachia. Groundwork was being laid for them to build in many other cities, but the process was a struggle. They found a successful formula for the goal—offer home ownership to low income people who are able to make a small house payment. Build low-cost housing using volunteer labor while involving the future homeowner in the building process. Finally, create no-interest loans to finance the house. It was an inspired idea and it caught on.

To reach the world, however, the Fullers knew they would have to take Habitat to a whole new level. From their headquarters in the town of Americus in Southern Georgia, the Fullers saw a possibility. Ten miles away in the tiny town of Plains was a man who might be able to help them—Jimmy Carter. The former U. S. President had spoken at a couple of Habitat functions. Following Carter's speech in 1983, Millard Fuller got the idea to approach Carter about helping the project along, and in early 1984, they made contact. When Carter said he was very interested in Habitat for Humanity, Fuller decided to boldly propose a list of fifteen possible roles the former president could take, hoping he would agree to one or two. His list included serving on Habitat's board, making media contacts, helping to raise money, doing a thirty-minute video, and working on a building crew for a day. To Fuller's surprise, Carter did not agree to do one or two items on the list; he agreed to do everything on the list.

Ironically, the task that captured the attention of the public most was Carter's willingness to serve on a building crew and to swing a hammer to help construct a house. At first, people thought Carter would just stop by for brief publicity photos, but the former president put together a work crew, traveled with them via bus to the Brooklyn, New York building site, worked tenaciously every day for a week, and slept in a church basement along with everyone else. That first time was in 1984. Carter has raised a team and served in a similar fashion every year since then and his dedicated service has attracted people from every walk of life to serve in similar roles.

So far, Habitat and its volunteers have built more than eight hundred thousand houses, sheltering more than five million people all over the world. Why? Because they, like former President Jimmy Carter, wanted to be a part of something bigger than themselves. They, like former President Jimmy Carter, believe in the importance of the common good.

THE GIFT

It was a warm summer day when God placed it in her hands. She trembled with emotion as she saw how fragile it appeared. This was a very special gift God was entrusting to her. A gift that would one day belong to the world. Until then, God instructed her, she was to be its guardian and protector. The woman said she understood and reverently took it home. She was determined to live up to the faith God had placed in her.

At first, she barely let it out of her sight, protecting it from anything she perceived to be harmful to its well-being; watching with fear in her heart when it was exposed to the environment outside of the sheltered cocoon she had formed around it. But the woman began to realize that she could not shelter it forever. It needed to learn to survive the harsh elements in order to grow strong. So with gentle care, she gave it more space to learn and grow.

Sometimes in bed at night, the feeling of inadequacy would overwhelm her. She wondered if she was capable of handling the awesome responsibility placed on her. Then she would hear the quiet whisper of God reassuring her that he knew she was doing her best. And she would fall asleep feeling comforted.

The woman grew more at ease with her responsibility as the years passed. The gift had enriched her life in so many ways. She could no longer remember what her life had been like before receiving it, nor imagine what life would be like without it. She had all but forgotten her agreement with God.

One day she became aware of how much the gift had

changed. It no longer had a look of vulnerability about it. Now it seemed to glow with strength and steadiness, almost as if it were developing a power within. Month after month, she watched as it became stronger and more powerful, and the woman remembered her promise. She knew deep within her heart that her time with the gift was nearing an end.

The inevitable day arrived when God came to take the gift and present it to the world. The woman felt a deep sadness, for she would miss its constant presence in her life. With heartfelt gratitude, she thanked God for allowing her the privilege of watching over the precious gift for so many years. Straightening her shoulders, she stood proud, knowing that it was indeed, a very special gift, one that would add to the beauty and essence of the world around it.

And the mother let her child go.

THE RESPECTABLE FISH

Once upon a time there was a Respectable Fish living in a respectable river. Every day he rose early and did all the things respectable fish do. He sent his fish kids off to a respectable fish school. He worked long and hard at a respectable fish job. He paid a respectable amount of fish taxes. And every Sunday morning he could be found in the front pew of First Fish Church at the corner of Third and Main. He was, quite simply, a very Respectable Fish.

One day, this Respectable Fish was swimming along the bank of the respectable river in which he lived when he spotted a respectable worm. The worm was dangling just below the surface of the water. He thought to himself, "That's a respectable worm. I'm a respectable fish. It must be for me. I think I'll have lunch! It is providence that I should be fed so well. After all, I am a rather respectable fish."

Without so much as another thought, the Respectable Fish gulped down the respectable worm. At that moment, he felt the most terrible pain he had ever felt in his life! It was a stabbing, piercing pain in his jaw. Frightened, he swam to the river bottom and kicked up some mud. He swam to the left bank and then to the right. He shot up above the water and went through all manner of wild gyrations. He tugged and jerked about. But with each tug the pain only increased. Then he realized he was hooked!

Meanwhile, all the other respectable fish watched with alarm. The change in their old friend was most unsettling. After a while, one of the other respectable fish spoke up and said, "I've never seen him act like this before."

A second one stated, "Me neither."

A third one chimed in, "Do you suppose he is not the respectable fish we thought he was?"

No one could see the fishing line in the water and no one took the time to discover the hook in his mouth.

MODUPE

Once there was a village in Nigeria, West Africa, where the people made their living by farming. The village lay in a large green valley lined with palm trees and bushes. Surrounding the village were fields dotted with crops of yams, corn, and other vegetables. Just beyond the fields was a deep river the villagers called Baba, which means father. The river was a friend and a provider for the people. The men used it for fishing, the women washed clothes on its banks, and the children played in its waters. In the rainy season, the river overflowed and the people were fearful of its power. Thus, in a place where the river wound beyond the fields, they built a strong dam to hold back the water.

There was a man in the village named Modupe, which means, "I am grateful." Modupe was a shy, quiet man whose wife had died and his children were all married. After his wife's death, he had moved to the top of the mountain overlooking the valley and lived alone. There, he had built a small hut and cleared a small piece of land to grow his vegetables. The people did not see Modupe very often, but they loved and respected him because he had the gift of healing the sick and because he was one of them.

One year at harvest time, there were unusually heavy rains, but the crops had done well and there was much to do. No one paid much attention to the heavy rains. As Modupe stood by his house on the mountain, he noticed that the river had become swollen from the rains and was straining the dam. He knew by the time he could run down to the village to warn the people of the flood, it would be too late and all would be lost. Even as

Modupe watched, the wall of the dam began to break and the water started to seep through.

Modupe thought of his friends in the village, their crops, their homes, their very lives were in danger if he did not find a way to warn them. Then an idea came to him. He rushed to his small hut and set it afire. When the people in the valley saw Modupe's house burning, they said, "Our friend is in trouble. Let's sound the alarm and go help him." Then, according to custom, men, women, and children ran up the mountain to see what they could do. When they reached the top of the hill, they did not have time to ask what had happened. A loud crashing noise behind them made them turn around and look down into the valley. The houses, their temple, and their crops were being destroyed by the river, which had broken the dam and was flooding the valley.

The people were, understandably, upset at their loss. But Modupe comforted them, "Don't worry," he said. "My crops are still here. We can share them while we build a new village." Then all the people began to sing and give thanks because they remembered that in coming to help a friend, they had saved their own lives.

THE GOOSE AND
THE GOLD EGG

Once upon a time there was a farmer who went to market and bought a goose. Arriving home he placed the goose in the goose house. The next morning the farmer checked on the goose. To his surprise, he discovered the goose had laid a single, gold egg. The next day, the farmer checked the nest again and found a second solid gold egg. The third day he checked the goose nest with great excitement. To his delight, he discovered yet another gold egg. Three gold eggs, one a day for three days!

Now, the farmer began to think about how he might increase production. With some thought and planning he developed his own mini process improvement. He began with the feed. He experimented with a variety of feed. He tried corn, wheat, rice and table scrapes. No matter what he fed the goose, production remained the same ... one solid gold egg every twenty-four hours.

With his feeding strategy having failed, he turned his attention to the nest. He experimented with several varieties of nesting materials. He tried cotton, including fine Egyptian cottons, Italian silks, various grasses, and even smooth pebbles from the creek. Once again, production remained the same. The goose produced one gold egg a day.

Time passed and a year came full circle. The farmer was both rich and frustrated. All his efforts to increase production had failed. The morning of the three-hundred and sixty-sixth day the farmer went out to check on the goose and his latest experiment. When he saw one gold egg in the nest, he became very angry. He tossed the gold egg over into a basket overflowing with gold eggs and exclaimed, "I've had enough! I will kill this goose, cut it open, and take out all the gold eggs and be done with this goose!"

So that is what he did. The farmer killed the goose that laid the gold eggs. He cut it open. He peered inside. Sadly, he did not find any gold eggs. It was then that he realized the goose was only capable of producing one gold egg every twenty-four hours.

STANDING YOUR GROUND

In the 1960s, drug companies were presenting nearly seven hundred applications a year to the Federal Drug Administration for new medicines. The beleaguered new drug section only had sixty days to review each drug before giving approval or requesting more data. A few months after Dr. Frances Kelsey joined the FDA, an established pharmaceutical firm in Ohio applied for a license to market a new drug, Kebadon. In liquid form, the drug seemed to relieve nausea in early pregnancy. It was given to millions of expectant women, mostly in Europe, Asia, and Africa. Although scientific studies revealed harmful side effects, the pharmaceutical firm printed 66,957 leaflets declaring its safety. The company exerted great pressure on Dr. Kelsey to give permission for labels to be printed in anticipation of the drug's approval. Dr. Kelsey reviewed the data and said "No."

Through several rounds of application, she continued to find the data "unsatisfactory." After a fourteen-month struggle, the company withdrew its application. Kebadon was thalidomide and by that time, the horror of thalidomide deformities was becoming well publicized. One firm decision by Dr. Kelsey spared untold agony in the United States. She had the strength to say no when no was necessary.

THE WAY YOU SAY IT

Walking into a noisy classroom, the teacher slapped her hand on the desk and sharply ordered, "I demand pandemonium." The class quieted down immediately. "It isn't what you demand," she later explained, "but the way you demand it." It is not always what you say, but the way you say it. For example, try saying, "I love you," with a scowl.

An international tourist came upon a group of people listening to an orator in the central square of a small European town. The speaker shouted from a makeshift podium. At one point, his arms waved about wildly, his stern face turned red, and the veins in his neck were bulging. To the stranger who could not speak his language, the man just seemed generally angry. Mingling with the crowd until he found someone who could speak his language, the man curiously asked what the speaker was ranting about.

The townsman responded by pointing to a church spire in the distance and said, "See that church steeple. The fellow who is speaking in the square is the pastor of that church. Right now, he is preaching about the love of God. Most of us are having a bit of trouble with the disconnect between how angry he seems and the love he's talking about."

UNPURCHASEABLE PEOPLE

An educator used to say that no society can last long unless it has a quorum of "unpurchaseable people." These are people of principle who cannot be bought, people who have learned to say no. I believe that these so-called unpurchaseable people are the truly contented and fulfilled souls among us.

Arthur MacArthur, Douglas MacArthur's father, told his son of such an unpurchaseable man. This man was a Union general in charge of the occupied territory surrounding New Orleans toward the end of the American Civil War. He was pressed by local plantation owners to permit them to haul their cotton to the wharfs. There the cotton could be sold for shipment to England. The general controlled all the wagons and horses and his orders were clear: the cotton crop would not get to market.

One day when Colonel Arthur MacArthur was visiting the general, two Southern ladies were ushered into the general's office, a "grand dame" and a beautiful young companion. The older lady came right to the point. She said the landowners needed the temporary use of transport facilities to move their cotton. The north did not wish to force England into the war, she argued, and was allowing some merchant ships to slip through the blockade. Therefore, the general should not oppose the sale of cotton for English textile mills. To show her gratitude, she handed over two hundred dollars in gold certificates. "And if you need other enticements, this young lady will supply them," she added. Then the two ladies left with the general holding the beautiful young woman's address.

The general immediately ordered MacArthur to dispatch this message to Washington. "To the President of the United States. I have just been offered two hundred dollars and the most beautiful woman I have ever seen to betray your trust. I am depositing the money with the Treasury of the United States and request immediate relief from this command. These people are simply getting too close to my price."

FAULTY MOTIVATION

Once upon a time there was a man who owned a company known throughout the land as U. S. Widgets, Inc. As owner and company president, Joe felt it was his responsibility to motivate his staff to ever-higher levels of performance. He decided to begin with his plant manager.

One clear afternoon, Joe took Jerry, his plant manager, out to a tall mountain overlooking the town. "Jerry," Joe began, "do you see that small rise down there just to the left of the town square?"

"Yes," responded Jerry. "It looks like it would be a lovely place to build a house. And what a view such a house would have."

"Exactly," answered Joe. "Jerry, I want you to stand very still and imagine a beautiful house sitting there on the rise overlooking the town. I also want you to imagine a big swimming pool to the left of the house. And, I want you to imagine a tennis court to the right of the house. Jerry, do you have all of that clearly pictured in your mind?"

"Yes," Jerry, the plant manager, answered.

"Well," said Joe, the president and owner, "if you work real hard and long next year and do an outstanding job, I'll be able to build me a house just like that."

WILLIAM TELL

The people of Switzerland were not always as free and happy as they are today. Many years ago, a proud tyrant named Gessler ruled over them and made their lives unpleasant.

One day this tyrant set up a tall pole in the public square and put his own cap on top of it. Then he gave orders that every man who came into his town should bow down before it. But there was one man named William Tell who would not bow to the tyrant's hat.

He stood straight with folded arms and laughed at the swinging cap. He would not bow down to Gessler.

When Gessler heard about William's refusal, he was very angry. He was afraid that other men would follow William's lead. Soon the whole country would rebel against him. So he made up his mind to punish William Tell.

William Tell's home was in the mountains, and he was a famous hunter. No one in all the land could shoot a bow and arrow as well as William. Gessler knew this, and so he devised a cruel plan to make the hunter's skill bring him grief. He ordered William Tell's son to stand in the public square with an apple on his head. He then demanded Tell shoot the apple with one of his arrows.

Tell pleaded with the tyrant to find another way to test his skill. What if the boy moves? What if the arrow does not carry straight and true?

"Will you make me kill my son?" he said.

"Say no more," said Gessler. "You must hit the apple with your arrow. If you refuse, my soldiers shall kill the boy."

Then, without another word, Tell fitted the arrow to his bow. He took aim, and let it fly. The boy stood firm and still. He was not afraid. He had great faith in this father's skill.

The arrow whistled through the air. It struck the apple in the center and carried it away. The people shouted and applauded Tell's skill.

As Tell was turning away, an arrow, which he had hidden under his coat, dropped to the ground.

"Why do you have this second arrow? What were you going to do with it?" The tyrant demanded?

Tell's answer was simple and clear. "This arrow was for you. If my son had been harmed, your life would have been forfeited."

ALEXANDER FLEMING

We owe the invention of the first antibiotic to an accident. In a small room at St. Mary's Hospital in London, Dr. Alexander Fleming experimented with bacteria from hospital patients. The boiler in the room next to his laboratory threw off so much heat that he often had to open a window, allowing dust and mold to enter.

On September 28, 1928, yet another petri dish with staphylococcus was contaminated by mold. Dr. Fleming was about to clean the dish when he noticed the bacteria around the green mold had disappeared. The mold appeared to release a substance which could kill bacteria! Fleming called the substance "penicillin."

Thanks to this happy accident, the discovery led to the development of other antibiotics thus ending the era when people died of simple bacterial infections. Every person who ever had their life saved by an antibiotic gladly applauds Dr. Fleming's happy accident.

MARVIN PIPKIN

Marvin Pipkin was a legendary engineer at General Electric. When he first got started at GE, a few of the other engineers decided to play a joke on him. They gave Pipkin this assignment: figure out a way to "frost" electric light bulbs from the inside.

To the other engineers, this was an impossible task. They watched with amusement as Pipkin set about trying to accomplish the task. Not knowing that the task was supposed to be impossible, Pipkin went right to work.

Pipkin not only figured out a way to frost bulbs from the inside, but also came up with a way to give the bulbs added strength—all in a single step!

A LEADER'S HEART

Shortly before Booker T. Washington became head of the Tuskegee Institute of Alabama, he was walking past the home of a wealthy family. The woman of the house, assuming Washington was one of the yard workers her husband had hired, asked him if he would chop some wood for her. Professor Washington smiled, nodded, took off his coat, and chopped the wood. When he carried the armload of wood into the woman's kitchen, a servant girl recognized him and rushed to her mistress to tell her of his identity.

The next morning, the woman appeared in Washington's office. Apologizing profusely, she said repeatedly, "I did not know it was you I put to work."

Washington replied with grace and generosity, "It's entirely all right madam. I like to work and I'm delighted to do favors for my friends and neighbors."

The woman was so taken with his goodwill and willingness to forgive she gave generous gifts to the institute and persuaded many of her wealthy friends to do so as well. In the end, Washington raised as much money for the institute from one act of chopping wood as he did from any other fundraising event.

Leaders are well-served by a small ego and big heart. The willingness to serve others is the essence of true leadership.

A FREE AND GRATEFUL NATION

When U.S. Army General H. Norman Schwarzkopf was a colonel stationed in Vietnam, he commanded the First Battalion of the Sixth Infantry. This unit had previously been known as the "Worst of the Six," but Schwarzkopf turned it around with strong leadership. After he improved the battalion, he was reassigned to a place Schwarzkopf described as "a horrible, malignant place," called the Batangan Peninsula. It was an area that had been fought over for thirty years, was covered with mines and booby traps, and was the site of numerous weekly casualties from those devices.

Schwarzkopf made the best of a bad situation. He introduced procedures to greatly reduce casualties and whenever a soldier was injured by a mine, he flew out to check on the man, evacuated him using his personal chopper, and talked to the other men to boost their morale.

On May 23, 1970, a man was injured by a mine and Schwarzkopf flew to where he lay. While Schwarzkopf's helicopter was evacuating the soldier, another man stepped on a mine severely injuring his leg. The man thrashed around on the ground screaming and wailing. That is when everyone realized that the first mine had not been a lonely booby trap. They were, in fact, standing in the middle of a minefield. Schwarzkopf believed the injured man could survive and even keep his leg, but only if he stopped flailing around. There was only one thing Schwarzkopf could do. He had to go to the man and immobilize him.

In his autobiography, *It Doesn't Take a Hero*, Schwarzkopf

wrote, "I started through the mine field one slow step at a time, staring at the ground, looking for telltale bumps or little prongs sticking up from the dirt. My knees were shaking so hard that each time I took a step; I had to grab my leg and steady it with both hands before I could take another. It seemed like a thousand years before I reached the kid." The two-hundred-pound Schwarzkopf, who had been a wrestler at West Point, then penned the wounded man and calmed him down. It saved the man's life and eventually, with the help of an engineer team, Schwarzkopf was able to get him and the others out of the minefield.

Later that night when Schwarzkopf was at the hospital, three black soldiers stopped him in a hallway and said, "Colonel, we saw what you did for the brother out there. We will never forget that and we will make sure that all the other brothers in the battalion know what you did."

Until that moment, it had not occurred to Schwarzkopf the soldier he had saved was black. For Schwarzkopf, all that mattered was the promise he had made to his men the day they deployed to Vietnam: "I will do all within my power to bring you home alive—it is the least an officer can do on behalf of a free and grateful nation."

Growth

Spark!

THE CHOICE

Once upon a time, there was a wise man who lived in a small village. Even though he did not think of himself as a wise man, his neighbors considered him a wise man. When they went to him for advice, he gave them very good advice.

Living in the same village was a young man who was certain the wise man was not so wise at all. Not only did he think the wise man was not so wise, but he felt it was his responsibility to demonstrate how foolish the old man really was.

The young man thought about the old man for a few days and hatched a plan. "I'll go to the wise man," the young man said to himself, "when he is giving advice in the public square. I will hold out to him a live bird cupped between my hands. And I will ask him, 'O wise one, tell me, is the bird I hold between my hands dead or alive?' If he says the bird is alive, I will crush it and show him a dead bird. If, on the other hand, he says the bird is dead, I will open my hands and let the bird fly away. No matter how the old man responds, he will be wrong and everyone will see just how foolish the old guy really is."

True to his plan, the young man waited until an afternoon when the wise man was in the public square giving advice. When the young man was satisfied the crowd had peaked, he approached the wise man. "O wise one, is the bird I hold between my hands dead or alive?"

The wise man looked the young man over thoughtfully as he considered the question. After a moment, the wise man positioned himself so he could look the young man level in the eye. Then, placing his hand atop the cupped hands of the young man, the wise man responded, "Is the bird dead or alive? It is up to you," said the wise man. "It is your choice."

THE FRIED FISH SHOP

Once upon a time there was a young man who lived in a second story apartment above a fried fish shop. He was a student with so little money all he could afford to eat each day was a single bowl of rice. Each day when he ate his bowl of rice, he would open all the windows of his second story apartment. The aroma of fried fish would drift up from the restaurant below and was so intense, it was almost as though he had fish to eat with his rice.

One day the young man was talking with a friend as they stood in front of the fried fish shop. He explained that his financial situation only allowed him a single bowl of rice each day, so he opened all the windows of his apartment to allow the smell of the fish to drift upward. The aroma was so intense that it was as if he had fish to eat.

As the young man was explaining his meal-time ritual, the owner of the fried fish shop ran out onto the sidewalk. The owner grabbed the young man by the arm and announced, "You can't smell the aroma of my fish frying without paying me something. I think I'm owed something for the smell of my fish."

The young man looked at him in amazement and responded, "You must be joking. If I had money to pay for the smell, I'd buy the fish." They argued back and forth for a while, the young man insisting he would not pay, and the owner of the fried fish shop insisting he should pay.

Finally, the owner of the fried fish shop said, "Okay, if you won't pay me, I'll sue you." The owner did sue and they landed in court. They each explained their position to the judge. The owner of the fried fish shop said to the judge, "He's been enjoying the aroma of my fish and I feel I'm owed something for it."

The young man countered, "Judge, if I could afford to pay for the smell, I'd buy the fish."

The judge responded, "Let me think about the matter for a moment."

She went into her chambers and after about twenty minutes returned. The judge turned to the owner of the fried fish shop and said, "I've decided you're due something for the smell of your fish." Then she turned to the young man and asked, "Do you have any money, any money at all?"

The young man replied, "Well, I have these few coins I've been saving to pay my tuition."

The judge said, "Let me have them." So the young man gave the coins to the judge who took them and dropped them several times from one hand to the other. The coins made the kind of clinking sound coins make when they bump together. Then the judge handed the coins back to the young man.

The owner of the fried fish shop protested. "Judge, I thought you said I was due something for the smell of my fish."

The judge responded, "I did and you've been paid. I've decided that the price of the smell of fish is the sound of money."

WE TAKE OUR
ATTITUDE WITH US

Once upon a time there was a small-town gas station owner. Each day, he would sit outside his gas station in his rocking chair. This was his way of welcoming motorists as they passed through his town. On this day, his granddaughter knelt at the foot of his chair playing as she slowly passed the time with him. As they watched the people come and go, a tall man, who surely had to be a visitor since they knew everyone in town, began looking around as if he were checking out the area for a place to live. The stranger walked up and asked, "So what kind of town is this we're in?"

The older gentleman slowly turned to the man and replied, "What kind of town are you from?"

The tourist said, "In the town I'm from, everyone is very critical of each other. The neighbors gossip about each other and it's a real negative place to live. I'm sure glad to be leaving. It's not a very cheerful place."

The old man, seated in his rocking chair, looked at the stranger and replied, "You know, that's just the kind of town this is."

An hour or so later, another family stopped for gas as they were passing through town. The car slowly turned in and rolled to a stop in front of the old gentleman and his granddaughter. The mother jumped out with two small children and asked where the restrooms were located. The man in the chair pointed to a small bent sign hanging by a single nail on the side of a door.

Then the father stepped out of the car: "Is this town a pretty good place to live?"

The old man replied, "What about the town you're from? How was it?"

The father looked at him and said, "Well, in the town I'm from, everyone is very close and always willing to lend their neighbor a helping hand. There's also a hello and thank you everywhere you go. To tell you the truth, I hate to leave. I feel like we are leaving family."

The older gentleman turned to the father and gave him a warm smile. "You know, that's a lot like this town."

The family returned to their car, said their thanks, waved goodbye, and drove away. Once the family was in the distance, the granddaughter looked up at her grandfather and asked, "Grandpa, how come when the first man came into our town, you told him it was a terrible place to live and when that family came into town, you told them it was a wonderful place to live?"

The grandfather replied, "Honey, you always find what you're looking for because you take your attitude with you everywhere you go."

A LITTLE HELP FROM MY FRIENDS

A man's car once stalled in heavy, Friday evening traffic just as the light turned green. All his efforts to start the engine failed. A chorus of honking rose from the cars behind him. Feeling just as frustrated as other drivers, eager to get home or to their weekend destinations, he got out of his car and walked back to the driver immediately behind him.

Calmly, he made a request: "I'm sorry, but I can't seem to get my car started. If you'll go up there and give it a try, I'll stay here and blow your horn for you."

HABITS

A yogi at an ashram found the presence of a stray cat annoying. The cat was particularly disruptive during the daily meditation sessions. It was true the cat was friendly and well-liked by all. It was also true his playful and amusing antics were a distraction for most of the students.

After many attempts to find a solution, the one that worked best was placing the cat in a crate with a saucer of milk. So each day, just prior to the call to meditation, the cat was placed in the crate where he drank the milk and promptly fell asleep. This practice soon became a routine and the routine became a habit. The ritual continued for many years until the cat passed away from old age.

The next day before meditation began, someone said, "We must find a cat to put in the crate."

"Why?" a new participant responded.

"Because it's always done that way," came the chorus from the students who had been there for many years.

The issue was put to an urgent vote and the spiritual value of the cat was confirmed. Within days another cat was acquired and the ritual of *the cat, the crate, and daily meditation* resumed.

STARFISH

Along the coast of the vast Atlantic Ocean, there lived an old man. Each day when the tide went out, he would make his way along the beach for miles. A neighbor would occasionally watch as the old man vanished into the distance and then later returned. The neighbor also noticed that, as he walked, the old man would often stoop down to lift something from the sand and then toss it away into the water.

One day when the old man went down to the beach, the neighbor followed wanting to satisfy his curiosity. Sure enough, as he watched, the old man bent down and gently lifted something from the sand and threw it into the ocean. By the time the old man made his next stop, the neighbor had come near enough to see he was picking up a starfish. The starfish, stranded by the retreating tide, would, of course, die of dehydration before the tide returned.

As the old man turned to return it to the ocean, the neighbor called out mockingly, "Hey old timer, what are you doing? This beach goes on for hundreds of miles and thousands of starfish get washed up every day. Surely you don't think throwing a few back is going to make a difference?"

The old man listened and paused for a moment, then held the starfish in his hand out toward his neighbor. Then he turned and tossed it into the ocean. "I think I made a difference for that one," he said.

TWO BROTHERS

In 1930, two brothers named Dick and Maurice moved from New Hampshire to California. They were in search of the American dream. Having just graduated from high school they saw few opportunities back home. So they headed straight for Hollywood where they eventually found jobs on a movie studio set. After a while, their entrepreneurial spirit and interest in the entertainment industry prompted them to open a theater in Glendale. But despite all their efforts, the brothers just could not make the business profitable. In the four years they ran the theater, they were unable to consistently generate enough money to pay their $100 a month rent.

The brothers' desire for success was strong, so they kept looking for better business opportunities. In 1937, they finally found something that worked. They opened a small drive-in restaurant in Pasadena located just east of Glendale. People in Southern California had become dependent on their cars and business was changing to accommodate this change. Drive-in restaurants sprang up in the early thirties and they were becoming ever more popular.

Rather than being invited into a dining room to eat, customers would drive into a restaurant parking lot, place their orders with car hops, and receive their food on trays right in their cars. The food was served on china plates complete with glassware and metal utensils. It was a timely idea in a society that was becoming faster paced and increasingly mobile. Dick and Maurice's tiny drive-in restaurant was a great success. In

1940, they decided to move the operation to San Bernardino, a boomtown fifty miles east of Los Angeles. They built a larger facility and expanded their menu. In addition to hot dogs, fries, and shakes, they served barbequed beef and pork sandwiches. A year or so later they added hamburgers. Their business exploded! Annual sales reached $200,000: more money than the two brothers ever imagined they might make.

In 1948, their intuition told them that the times were changing and they made modifications to their restaurant business. They eliminated the carhops, started serving only walk-up customers, and streamlined everything. The brothers reduced their menu and focused on selling hamburgers. They eliminated plates, glassware, and metal utensils switching to paper products instead. They reduced their cost and the prices they charged customers. They also created what they called the *speedy-service system*. Their kitchen became an assembly line where each person focused on service, quality, and speed. Their goal was to fill every customer's order in thirty seconds or less, and they succeeded.

Who were these brothers? Back in those days you could have found out by driving to their restaurant on the corner of Fourteenth and E Streets in San Bernardino. On the front of their small building hung a neon sign: *McDonald's Hamburgers.*

LYDIA WILLIAMS

Lecturer, Charles Hobbs, told a story about a woman who lived in London over a century ago. She saved what little money she could working as a maid and used it one evening to hear a famous speaker of her day. His speech moved her deeply and she waited to visit with him afterward. "How fine it must be to have had the opportunities you have had in life," she said.

"My dear lady," he replied, "have you ever received an opportunity?"

"Not me, I have never had a chance," she said.

"What do you do?" the speaker asked.

She answered, "I peel onions and potatoes in my sister's boarding house."

"How long have you been doing this?" he pursued.

"Fifteen miserable years."

"And where do you sit?" he continued.

"Why, on the bottom step in the kitchen." She looked puzzled.

"And where do you put your feet?"

"On the floor," she answered becoming even more puzzled.

"What is the floor?"

"It is glazed brick."

Then he said, "My dear lady, I will give you an assignment. I want you to write me a letter about the brick."

Against her protest about being a poor writer, he made her promise to complete the assignment.

The next day as she sat down to peel onions and potatoes, she gazed at the brick floor. That evening, she pulled one loose, took it to a brick factory, and asked the owner to explain to her how bricks were made. Still not satisfied, she went to a library and found a book on bricks. She learned that one hundred twenty different kinds of bricks and tile were being produced in England at that time. She discovered how clay beds, which existed for millions of years, were formed. Her research captivated her imagination and she spent every spare moment learning more. She returned to the library night after night and this woman, who never had a chance, gradually began to learn.

After several weeks of study, she set out to write her letter as promised. She sent a thirty-six-page document about the brick in her kitchen, and to her surprise, she received a letter back. Enclosed was a payment for her research. He had published her letter. And along with the money came a new assignment. This time, he asked her to write about what she found underneath the brick.

For the first time in her life, she could hardly wait to get back to the kitchen. She pulled up the brick and there was an ant. She held it in her hand and examined it. That evening, she hurried back to the library to study ants. She learned that there were hundreds of different kinds of ants. Some were so small they could stand on the head of a pin, while others were so large, one could feel the weight of them in one's hand. She started her own ant colony and examined ants underneath a lens.

Several months later, she wrote her findings in a three-hundred-fifty-page "letter." It too was published. She soon quit her kitchen job to take up writing. Before she died, she had traveled to the lands to which she had always wanted to travel and experienced more than she ever imagined possible. And this, of course, was the woman who had never had a chance.

Her name: Lydia Williams, a science writer for the London Times.

HANG IN THERE

The owner of a hair salon in a small town enjoyed the serenity of knowing that he was the only salon in town. He was responsible for cutting and styling the hair of just about every person in town. His income allowed him to live comfortably and to send all six of his children to college.

Unfortunately for him, big business came to his town. Right across the street from his busy little hair salon, sprang up one of those new full-service salon franchises.

Immediately, the media campaign began; ads in the newspapers, magazines, and billboards announced, "Everything for $10! $10 haircuts, $10 perms, $10 manicures, everything for $10."

Soon his customers began visiting the salon across the street and the man's business sat empty.

Desperate, he hired an expensive consultant. "I'm finished," he cried. "It's impossible for me, little me, to compete with them."

The consultant squinted his eyes at the salon across the street. "Not just yet," he responded. With that, the consultant picked up the phone and dialed the town's only billboard company.

"Yes, on top of our salon ... big letters ... the message? 'We fix $10 haircuts.'"

THE BLACKSMITH

Once upon a time there was a blacksmith who lived in a small village. The blacksmith took great pride in his work. He was so proud of the swords, the plough shares, and the chains which he manufactured. He engraved his initials into every item so that anytime an item came back to him, he would know that he had made it. Very few came back to him because he manufactured such high-quality items.

As time passed, the town in which he lived was conquered by an invading army and the blacksmith was thrown into a dungeon. He was shackled with heavy chains. But this did not concern him for he was a powerful, strong man and he knew all about chains. He was confident that by finding the weakest link and exacting enough pressure on it, he could break loose and make his way to freedom. When he passed the chain through his hands, however, he came upon the secret mark that told him he himself had forged the chain. He cried out in despair knowing that he would never be able to break the chain. It had no weak link. He was doomed to be held in bondage by a chain that he himself had forged.

VALENTINE'S DAY

Little Chad was a shy, quiet young man. One day he came home and told his mother that he would like to make a valentine for everyone in his class.

Her heart sank. She thought, "I wish he wouldn't do that," because she had watched the children when they walked home from school. Her Chad was always behind them. They laughed and hung on to each other and talked to each other. But Chad was never included.

Nevertheless, she decided she would go along with her son. So she purchased the paper, glue, and crayons. For three weeks, night after night, Chad painstakingly made thirty-five valentines.

Valentine's Day dawned, and Chad was beside himself with excitement. He carefully stacked them up, put them in a bag, and bolted out the door.

His mother decided to bake his favorite cookies and serve them nice and warm with a glass of milk when he came home from school. She just knew he would be disappointed and maybe that would ease the pain a little. It hurt her to think he would not get many valentines—maybe none at all.

That afternoon she had the cookies and milk on the table. When she heard the children outside, she looked out the window. Sure enough, there they came, laughing and having the best time. And, as always, there was Chad in the rear. He walked a little faster than usual. She fully expected him to burst into tears as soon as he came through the kitchen door. His arms were empty, she noticed, and when the door opened, she choked back the tears.

"Mommy has some cookies and milk for you," she said. But he hardly heard her words. He just marched right on by, his face aglow, and all he would say was: "Not a one. Not a one."

Her heart sank. And then he added, "I didn't forget a one, not a single one!"

STARTING OVER

He had been expelled from college and his attempts at business had failed. Now as he stood on the wind-swept shores of Lake Michigan one wintry night, the thirty-two-year-old man took one last look up at the sky as he prepared to jump into the icy water. It was an over-powering moment. He felt a rush of awe as he saw the starry heavens and the thought seared his mind. "You have no right to end your life. You do not belong to you."

Buck Fuller walked away from the lake and started over. From that point on, he embarked on a journey that led him into careers as an inventor, engineer, mathematician, architect, poet, and cosmetologist. He eventually won dozens of honorary degrees and a Nobel Prize nomination. Fuller invented the geodesic dome, wrote two-dozen books, circled the globe fifty-seven times, and told millions about his dreams for the future. He seldom repeated himself in lectures that sometimes lasted two to three hours on topics that ranged from education to the origin of life.

The day Richard Buckminster Fuller found hope was the day he looked beyond Buck Fuller to something larger than himself.

LET THE PAST BE THE PAST

It is difficult for most of us to forgive. It is difficult to let the past be past. We see this in the story of an elderly Virginia woman who had lived to see her beloved Richmond occupied by Union troops during the Civil War. The matron was walking down a Richmond street when she tripped over a step and fell. A Union soldier courteously helped her up. "How very kind of you, young man," she said acidly. "If there is a cool spot in hell, I hope you get it." Maybe it was still a bit early for her to let go of those deep-seated resentments, but angry and bitter lives are never happy lives.

There is a legend about an African tribe that ritualizes forgiveness. When a tribe member acts irresponsibly or unjustly, he or she is taken to the center of the village. All work ceases and every man, woman, and child in the village gathers in a large circle around the accused. Then the tribe bombards the rejected person with affirmations. One at a time, friends and families enumerate all the good the individual has done. Every incident and every experience that can be recalled with some detail is recounted. All their positive attributes, strengths, and kindnesses are recited carefully and at length. Finally, the tribal circle is broken, a joyous celebration takes place, and the outcast is welcomed back into the tribe.

EDDIE

When the twentieth century was new, a young boy quit school to help with the family expenses. When he was fifteen, he became interested in automobiles and worked in a garage. He subscribed to a correspondence course on automobiles. After a long day in the garage, he would spend the evening studying at his kitchen table. When he felt ready, he walked into the Miller Automobile Company of Columbus, Ohio.

When Mr. Miller noticed him, he asked, "Well, what do you want?"

"I just thought I would tell you I'm coming to work here tomorrow morning," the boy replied.

"Oh, who hired you?"

"Nobody yet, but I'll be on the job in the morning. If I'm not worth anything, you can fire me."

Early the next morning, the young man returned to the dealership. He noticed the floor was thick with metal shavings and accumulated dirt and grease. The boy picked up a broom and shovel and went to work cleaning the place.

Eddie Rickenbacker went on to excel in many fields, including automobile racing, piloting World War I planes, and founding what was to become one of America's largest commercial airlines, Eastern Airlines.

ROY RIEGELS

A grizzled old sea captain was often spotted by his crew opening a small, locked box on the bridge. He would peek inside at its contents then quickly close the lid before anyone could see inside. The crew's curiosity grew and on the day the captain retired, they rushed to the bridge, cut the lock, and looked inside the box. There they found a sheet of paper that read, "Left-Port. Right-Starboard."

Many of us have those moments when we are scared to death of making a mistake. And some people feel as if no one is ever paying attention until they do make a mistake. If you have goofed in a big way recently, maybe you need to hear about Roy Riegels.

Roy Riegels played in the 1929 Rose Bowl Championship football game between Georgia Tech and the University of California. Shortly before halftime, Roy Riegels made a huge mistake. He got the ball for California and somehow became confused and started running in the wrong direction. One of his teammates outdistanced him and tackled him after he had run sixty-five yards, just before he would have scored for the opposing team. Of course, Georgia Tech gained a distinctive advantage because of his error and they were more than a little pleased.

The men filed off the field into the locker room. All but Riegels sat down on the benches and on the floor. Riegels wrapped his blanket around his shoulders, sat in a corner, his face in his hands, and wept. Coach Nibs Price struggled with what to do with Roy. He finally looked at the team and said simply, "Men, the same team that played the first half will start the second."

All the players except Roy trotted out to the field. He would not budge. Though the coach looked back and called to him again and again, he remained huddled in the corner. Coach Price finally went over to him and said, "Roy, didn't you hear me?"

"Coach," he said, "I can't do it. I've ruined everything. I've ruined the school, I've ruined myself, I couldn't face that crowd in the stadium to save my life."

But Coach Price put his hand on Riegels's shoulder and said, "Roy, get up and go on back. The game is only half over."

Roy Riegels went out on the field and played with a zeal that no one had ever seen before. Roy was determined to deserve the goodwill the coach had extended to him after his colossal mistake.

A DEBT TO SOCIETY

James Carter left his rural Louisiana home at the age of thirteen to make his way in the world. What he found was a life of hard times, trouble, and eventually, jail. In 1959, Carter was serving a sentence of hard labor for theft in the Mississippi State Penitentiary. Today, he is a richer man because of that experience. By working on a chain gang in the hot Mississippi sun, Carter often sang to help pass the time and make the heat and hard work more bearable.

On one such occasion, musicologist, Alan Lomax, made a recording of Carter leading the work gang in the song, "Po Lazarus." Many decades later, during a visit to the Alan Lomax archives, music producer, T. Bone Burnette, heard this recording. He was overwhelmed by the sound of Carter's voice and the voices of the other prisoners as their sledge hammers pounded out the rhythms of the song. Burnette turned this original recording into the movie sound track of *O Brother, Where Art Thou.*

Carter has long since mended his ways and keeps a low profile. He is a retired shipping clerk who has lived in Chicago with his wife and three daughters since 1967. But Carter's life changed a bit when he received his first royalty check for twenty thousand dollars. A short time later Carter and his family attended the Grammy Awards. The *O Brother, Where Art Thou* sound track won six Grammies.

THE TIGER WHO THOUGHT
HE WAS A GOAT

Once upon a time a motherless tiger cub was adopted by a family of goats. The goats brought the tiger cub up to believe he should speak their language, emulate their ways, eat their food, and in general believe he was a goat himself.

Then one day a King Tiger came along. When all the goats scattered in fear, the young tiger was left alone to confront him. He was afraid and yet, somehow, not afraid. The King Tiger asked him what he meant by his unseemly masquerade. But all the young tiger could do in response was bleat nervously and continue nibbling at the grass.

Frustrated and angry, the King Tiger carried the young tiger to a pond. There he forced him to look at their two reflections side-by-side. When the young tiger failed to understand, the King Tiger offered him his first taste of raw meat. At first the young tiger recoiled from the unfamiliar taste. But as he ate more and began to feel it warming his blood, the truth gradually became clear to him. Lashing his tail and digging his claws into the ground, the young beast raised his head high, and the jungle trembled at the sound of his happy roar.

The King Tiger spoke once more: "Remember, my young friend, we do not see ourselves clearly until we see ourselves through the eyes of those who care."

THE FOX AND THE CROW

A crow sat high in a tree. Black and sleek and proud, he looked down upon the fox below. In the crow's mouth was a piece of cheese he had stolen from a nearby farmhouse. Meanwhile, the fox gazed up at the crow and wondered how he might persuade the crow to drop the cheese.

In a moment an idea came to the fox. The fox said to the crow, "My you are a beautiful bird. I suspect you are the most beautiful bird in the forest." Caught up in the fox's admiration, the crow preened and warmed to the praise.

Seeing his plan was working, the fox continued. "Yes, Mr. Crow, you are a beautiful bird. And you have a lovely voice. Whenever I hear sweet, melodious notes floating through the forest, I know you must be singing." Once again the crow preened.

And once again the fox continued, "Please, Mr. Crow, sing a tune for me. It would make my day if I could hear the melodious sound of your voice."

Without thought or hesitation, the crow dropped the cheese and began to sing. The fox caught the cheese and trotted away as the Crow continued to sing.

Having enjoyed the cheese, the fox could not help but recall his grandmother's counsel: *Pride goes before a fall.*

THE NORTH WIND
AND THE SUN

The north wind and the sun had a quarrel as to which of them was the stronger. While they were arguing with much heat and bluster, a traveler wrapped in a cloak passed along the road.

"Let us agree," said the Sun, "that he is the stronger who can strip that traveler of his cloak."

"Very well," growled the North Wind and at once sent a cold, howling blast against the traveler.

With the first gust of wind the traveler's cloak was all but torn from his body. But he immediately wrapped it closely around him. The harder the wind blew, the tighter he held it to him. The North Wind tore angrily at the cloak, but all his efforts were in vain.

Then the Sun began to shine. At first his beams were gentle, and in the pleasant warmth after the bitter cold of the North Wind, the traveler allowed his cloak to hang loosely from his shoulders. The sun's rays grew warmer and warmer till the man took off his cap and mopped his brow. A short time later, the traveler overheated. He pulled off his cloak and, to escape the blazing sun, threw himself down in the welcome shade of a roadside tree.

THE CROW AND THE PITCHER

Once there was a thirsty crow. She had flown a long way looking for water to drink. Suddenly she saw a pitcher. She flew down and saw it held a little water, but it was so low in the pitcher she could not reach it.

"But I must have that water," she cried. "I am too weary to fly farther. What can I do? I know! I'll tip the pitcher over."

She beat it with her wings, but it was too heavy. She could not move it.

Then she thought a while. "I know now! I will break it! Then I will drink the water as it pours out. How good it will taste!"

With beak and claws and wings she threw herself against the pitcher. But it was too strong.

The poor crow stopped to rest. "What am I going do? I cannot die of thirst with water so close. There must be a way."

After a while, the crow had a bright idea. There were many small stones lying about. She picked them up one by one and dropped them into the pitcher. Slowly the water rose, till at last she could drink it. The water tasted just as good as she knew it would!

"There is always a way to solve a problem," the crow thought to herself, "if only you take the time to find it."

Faith

Spark!

ERIC LIDDELL

In 1945 in a Japanese internment camp in China, a forty-three-year-old man did everything he could to lead and serve his fellow prisoners. Without the benefit of equipment or supplies, he taught science to many of the children in the make-shift school they created. He also taught Sunday school, led Bible studies for adults, and tended to the elderly and infirm. Along with teaching and assisting others, he organized youth sporting events to promote fitness and boost morale. In fact, he especially enjoyed helping the children with athletics because he had been an athlete himself, an especially well-known one in his native Scotland. Many years earlier, the people had called him "The Flying Scotsman" because of his prowess in track.

If you have seen the movie, *Chariots of Fire*, then you know his name: Eric Liddell. A one-hundred-meter sprinter by talent and training, he declined to run in that race during the Paris Olympics of 1924 when he learned it would be run on a Sunday. A devout Christian, he believed that running on Sunday violated the keeping of the Sabbath; something he would not do for king, country, or Olympic glory. For the stand he took, Eric Liddell was called a traitor.

Liddell refused to run in the one hundred meters; however, he got the opportunity to run in a four-hundred-meter race. Though he had not trained for that distance, he took the opportunity. Remarkably, he not only won, he set a world record in the process.

The welcome that Liddell received once back in England was incredible, but it was nothing compared to the celebration in his native Scotland. What was his response to his fame? He quietly finished his degree in science and divinity; then, he traveled to China as a missionary in 1925. For nearly twenty years, he worked with the Chinese people teaching, sharing his faith, and serving in numerous other ways.

In 1943, Eric Liddell found himself in a one-hundred-fifty by two-hundred-yard internment camp along with 1,800 other "enemy nationals." While there, he served everyone he could. The children were especially delighted with him. They had grown up hearing the story of the athlete who refused to run on Sunday. He gained not only the love of the children, but also that of the imprisoned adults and the respect and admiration of their Japanese captors.

If Liddell was in great pain in early 1945, he never really let on. Despite his illness, he simply continued his responsibilities of teaching and coaching the children. But on February 21, 1945, just months before the end of the war, he succumbed to an undetected brain tumor. He was laid to rest in a little cemetery outside the walls of the camp.

The record books may remember Eric Liddell, the runner, but the people whose lives he touched remember Eric Liddell, the leader.

JUDGE WEARING

Judge James Wearing was a part of what was called the "old families" of Charleston, South Carolina. His ancestors came to Charleston with the original grants made to the landed gentry of England in 1720. His family had been there when Charleston's first church was founded in 1754 and his family had been a member.

But years after the founding of the colony and years after the founding of that first congregation, Judge Wearing would make history in a way his ancestors could have never anticipated. In 1947, Judge Wearing handed down the first desegregation ruling issued by a judge in the United States. This was seven years before the famous *Brown vs. Board of Education* was issued by the U. S. Supreme Court in 1954. What happened following Judge Wearing's 1947 ruling would change his world and the world of his family forever.

In the days following his decision, the schools in Charleston had to be desegregated, and he faced what he could not have anticipated. First, he was assaulted in a public place by a man he had known all his life and had called a friend. He was the object of racial slurs and a cross was burned in his yard.

A few days after the cross was burned in his yard, the pastor and lay leaders of his church visited him in his courthouse office. They informed him they would like him and his family to leave the congregation. They were no longer welcome. Within a couple of weeks, his home was set afire. This became for Judge James Wearing the last straw. He moved his family to New York where he would live the balance of his life. He was literally run out of Charleston.

In 1969, Judge Wearing died and his last request was granted. His body was taken back to Charleston to be buried in the family plot where his ancestors had been buried for generations. By Judge Wearing's request, the following was inscribed beneath his name and birth and death dates: "To the citizens of Charleston, I forgive you even as God has forgiven me."

VAN GOGH

Vincent Van Gogh was not always an artist. In fact, he wanted to be a church pastor and he served as the pastor in a Belgium mining community, Borinage. He discovered the miners there endured deplorable working conditions and poverty level wages. Their families were malnourished and struggled simply to survive. The small salary he received from the church allowed him a moderate lifestyle, which, in contrast to the poor, seemed unfair.

One cold February evening while he watched the miners trudging home, he spotted an old man, wrapped in a burlap sack for warmth, staggering toward him across the fields. Van Gogh immediately laid his own clothing out on the bed, set aside enough for one change, and decided to give the rest away. He gave the old man a suit of clothes and he gave his overcoat to a pregnant woman whose husband had been killed in a mining accident. He lived on starvation rations and spent his salary on food for the miners. The children in one family contracted typhoid fever. Though feverish himself, he packed up his bed and took it to them.

A prosperous family in the community offered him free room and board, but Van Gogh declined the offer, stating that it was the final temptation he must reject if he was to faithfully serve this community of poor miners. He believed that if he wanted them to trust him, he must become one of them. And if they were to learn of the love of God through him, he must love them enough to share with them.

He was acutely aware of the wide chasm which can separate words and actions. He knew that people's lives often speak louder and clearer than their words. Maybe it was that same knowledge that led Francis of Assisi to frequently remind his monks, "Wherever you go, preach; use words if necessary."

PRAYING HANDS

About 1490, two young friends, Albrecht Durer and Franz Knigstein were struggling artists. Since both were poor, they worked to support themselves while they studied art. Work took so much of their time, advancement was slow. Finally, they reached an agreement. They would draw lots and one of them would work to support both of them while the other would study art.

Albrecht won and began to study while Franz worked at hard labor to support them. They agreed that when Albrecht was successful, he would support Franz who would then study art. Albrecht went off to the cities of Europe to study. As the world now knows, he had not only talent, but genius. When he had attained success, he went back to keep his bargain with Franz. But Albrecht soon discovered the enormous price his friend had paid. As Franz worked at hard manual labor to support his friend, his fingers had become stiff and twisted, his slender sensitive hands had been ruined for life. He could no longer execute the delicate brush strokes necessary for painting.

Though his artistic dreams could never be realized, he was not embittered. He celebrated his friend's success. One day Durer came upon his friend unexpectedly and found him kneeling with his gnarled hands intertwined in prayer. Albrecht Durer, the great genius, hurriedly sketched the folded hands of his faithful friend. A little later he completed the great masterpiece known as *The Praying Hands*. Today art galleries everywhere feature Albrecht Durer's works. This particular masterpiece tells an eloquent story of love, sacrifice, labor, and gratitude.

PACKING PARACHUTES

One organization that strives to match its people to the right job is the U. S. Military. This is particularly true now that it employs an all-volunteer force. If each function in the military command does not work well with all the other parts, terrible and even deadly events can occur.

Nobody is more keenly aware of this fact than a combat pilot. Take, for example, Charlie Plumb. He retired as a U. S. Navy captain. A graduate of Annapolis, he served in Vietnam in the mid 1960s, flying seventy-five missions from the aircraft carrier, U. S. Kitty Hawk.

On an aircraft carrier, you can readily observe how all the pieces of the military puzzle come together to support each other. A carrier is often described as a floating city with its crew of more than five thousand men and women. A carrier's population is greater than that of some towns in which its crew members grew up. It must be self-sustaining and each of its crew, in seventeen departments, must function as a team in order to accomplish its mission.

Every pilot knows of the team effort required to put a jet in the air. It takes hundreds of team members utilizing dozens of technical specialties to launch, monitor, support, land, and maintain an aircraft. Even more people are involved if that plane is armed for combat.

Charlie Plumb undoubtedly recognized many people worked tirelessly to keep him flying. But despite the efforts of the best-trained air support in the world, Plumb found himself in a North

Vietnamese prison as a POW after his F4 Phantom Jet was shot down on May 19, 1967, during his 75th mission. Plumb was held prisoner for nearly six grueling years, part of the time in the infamous Hanoi Hilton. During those years, he and his fellow prisoners were humiliated, starved, tortured, and forced to live in squalid conditions. Yet he did not let the experience break him. He now says, "Our unity through our faith and our love for our country were the great strength which kept us going through some very difficult times."

Plumb was released from his imprisonment on February 18, 1973, and continued his career in the Navy. But an incident that happened years after his return to the United States marked his life as surely as his imprisonment. One day, he and his wife, Kathy, were eating in a restaurant when a man came to the table and said, "You're Plumb. You flew jet fighters in Vietnam."

"That's right," answered Plumb, "I did."

"It was Fighter Squadron 114 on the Kitty Hawk. You were shot down. You parachuted into enemy hands," the man continued. "You spent six years as a prisoner of war."

The former pilot was taken aback. He looked at the man, trying to identify him, but could not. "How in the world did you know that?" Plumb finally asked.

"I packed your parachute," the man said.

Plumb was staggered. All he could do was struggle to his feet and shake the man's hand. "I must tell you," Plumb finally said, "I've said a lot of prayers of thanks for your nimble fingers, but I never thought I would have the opportunity to say thanks in person."

THE GREATNESS OF AMERICA

Early in the nineteenth Century, the French statesman, Alexander deTocqueville made a study of democracy in the United States. What follows is what he wrote about his observations.

I sought for the greatness and genius of America in her commodious harbors and her ample rivers and it was not there. I sought for the greatness and genius of America in her fertile fields and bounteous forests and it was not there.

I sought for the greatness and genius of America in her rich mines and her vast world commerce and it was not there.

I sought for the greatness and genius of America in her public school system and her institutions of learning and it was not there.

I sought for the greatness and genius of America in her democratic congress and her matchless constitution and it was not there.

Not until I went into the churches of America and heard her pulpits flame with righteousness did I understand the secret of her genius and power.

America is great because America is good and if America ever ceases to be good, America will cease to be great.

SARAJEVO

It was 1994. Daily, the city of Sarajevo was under siege. Mortars and artillery fire had transformed once beautiful buildings into rubble. Sarajevo citizens were frightened, weary, and increasingly despondent. Then, one February day, a mortar shell exploded in the market, killing sixty-eight civilians. Many more were wounded and maimed from the blast.

A cellist with the Sarajevo symphony could no longer stand the killing. He took his cello to the market, sat down amidst the rubble, and played a concert. When he finished, he simply took up his instrument and left. Every day for sixty-eight days, he came to the market. Every day, he played a concert. It was his gift of love to the city. He did it because he felt his community needed hope.

TOOLS FOR SALE

It was advertised that the devil was going to put his tools up for sale. On the date of the sale, the tools were displayed for public inspection; each tool being marked with its sale price.

There were a treacherous lot of implements: Hatred, Envy, Jealousy, Deceit, Lying, Pride, and so on. Laid apart from the rest was a harmless looking tool, well-worn and priced very high.

"What is the name of this tool?" asked one of the purchasers, pointing to it.

"That is Discouragement," the devil replied tersely.

"Why have you priced it so high?"

"Because it is more useful to me than the others. I can pry open and get inside a person's heart with that when I cannot get near him with my other tools. Once I get inside, I can make him do what I choose. That tool is badly worn because I use it on almost everyone. Most people don't even know Discouragement belongs to me."

THE STORY OF THE CHRISTMAS TREE

No one knows exactly how the Christmas tree custom began, but there are several legends surrounding it. One legend tells of Saint Boniface, an English monk, who organized the Christian Church in France and Germany. One day, in his travels, he came upon a group of pagan worshipers. They had gathered around a great oak tree to sacrifice a child to the god, Thor. To stop the sacrifice and save the child's life, the Saint flattened the oak with one blow of his fist. In its place, a small fir tree sprang up. The Saint told the pagans the tiny fir was the Tree of Life and represented the eternal life of Christ.

According to another legend, Martin Luther, the founder of the Protestant faith, was walking through the woods one Christmas Eve. It was clear and cold outside and the light from millions of stars was glimmering through the branches of the evergreen trees. Luther was so awed by the beauty of the sight he cut down a small tree and brought it home to his family. To recreate the effect of the starlight, he placed candles on its branches.

Yet another Christmas legend tells of a poor woodsman who was returning home on Christmas Eve long ago. He encountered a child who was lost and hungry. Despite his own poverty, the woodsman gave the child food and shelter for the night. When the woodsman woke up in the morning, he found a beautiful glittering tree outside his door. The hungry child was really the

Christ Child in disguise. He created the tree to reward the good man for his charity.

The actual origin of the Christmas tree may be the "Paradise Play." In medieval times, morality plays were performed all over Europe as a way of teaching the lessons of the Bible. The Paradise Play, which showed the creation of man and the fall of Adam and Eve from the Garden of Eden, was performed every year on December 24. An apple tree was a necessary prop, but because the play was performed in winter when all the fruit trees were bare, the actors used evergreens hung with apples.

The Christmas tree tradition first became popular in Germany in the sixteenth century. Devout Christians brought decorated trees into their homes. In areas where trees were scarce, families built Christmas pyramids instead: simple structures built of wood and decorated with evergreens and candles.

Soon, the Christmas tree became popular in other European countries. Prince Albert, the husband of Queen Victoria, popularized Christmas trees in England. In 1841, the royal couple decorated the first English Christmas tree at Windsor Castle with candles and a variety of sweets, fruits, and gingerbread.

In the 1850s, Charles Dickens described an English tree that was decorated with dolls, miniature furniture, tiny musical instruments, costume jewelry, toy guns and swords, fruit, and candy.

The first record of a Christmas tree on public display in the United States was in the 1830s. Because most Americans considered the tree to be an oddity, the German settlers of Pennsylvania put one on display to raise money for a local church. In 1851, a German minister set up a Christmas tree outside his church. The people in his parish were scandalized and asked him to take it down. They felt it was a return to pagan practices.

By the 1890s, however, American toy importers were bringing in Christmas ornaments from Germany, and the Christmas tree custom was becoming popular around the United States. There was one major difference between the European and American trees: the European tree was small, rarely more than four feet high, while the ideal American tree reached from floor to ceiling. In the early 1900s, Americans decorated their trees primarily with homemade ornaments. Apples, nuts, and almonds were traditional German-American ornaments, along with cookies in a variety of delightful shapes. Popcorn was dyed in bright colors and strung with tinsel and berries.

The invention of the electric bulb in the late nineteenth century made it possible for Christmas trees to glow with light for days on end. It was then community Christmas trees began to appear all over North America. Every Christmas, sixteen Irish yew trees sparkle on San Francisco's Union Square. At Rockefeller Center in New York, a giant tree gleams above the outdoor ice skating rink. In Washington, D.C., the President lights a tall spruce on the White House lawn; fifty large colored balls symbolize each state. For people in these and other cities, the tree lighting ceremony marks the beginning of the Christmas Season.

THE LEGEND OF SAINT NICHOLAS

Every Christmas, Santa Claus comes to millions of children around the world. To Americans, he comes from the North Pole in a sled pulled by his famous reindeer. To the Dutch, he comes by sea in a ship. On his way to visit German children, he rides through the air on a white horse. However he travels, Santa Claus brings gifts and joy everywhere he goes.

The tale of Santa Claus began with a man called Saint Nicholas, Bishop of Myra, who lived during the fourth century. Myra was in Asia Minor, a region that is now Turkey. Saint Nicholas was known for his wisdom and charity. Legend has it that he came from a wealthy family and gave all his money to the poor. Some claim that the Bishop could even perform miracles. He died around 340 A.D. and was buried in Myra.

In the year 1087, some religious sailors from the Italian region of Bari decided to take the remains of the Saint out of Asia Minor and bring them to Italy. So they built a church in their hometown to honor him. Bari, a port town in Southern Italy, once welcomed ships from all over Europe and the East. Soon, pilgrims from all over Christendom visited the Church of Saint Nicholas.

These pilgrims carried the image of Saint Nicholas back home to their native lands. The Russians called him their Patron Saint. They knew him as a bishop with his bishop's miter, red cape, and long white beard. For the Greeks, he became the Patron

Saint of Sailors; for the French, the Patron of Lawyers; and in Belgium, he was believed to be the helper of both travelers and children.

As early as the twelfth century, Saint Nicholas Day became a day for gift giving and charity; it became an official church holiday and feast day all over Europe. In Germany, France, and Holland, December 6 marked the time when religious people offered presents to children and to the poor. Every year, children would await the arrival of the Saint who rewarded them with gifts if they were good and punished them with a rod if they were bad.

The Dutch colonists took Saint Nicholas with them to America, where he was gradually transformed from an austere bishop to a jolly old elf. First, Washington Irving, of Sleepy Hollow fame, described the saint as a plump and jolly old Dutchman in his comic *History of New York*. The second step in Saint Nicholas' American transformation was brought about by a professor named Clement Clarke Moore. Moore, the father of several children, presented his family with a Christmas gift: the famous poem, *A Visit from St. Nicholas*, first published in 1823. This is how he described Saint Nicholas:

He had a broad face and little round belly,

That shook when he laughed, like a bowl full of jelly,

He was chubby and plump, a right jolly old elf,

And I laughed when I saw him, in spite of myself;

A wink of his eye and a twist of his head,

Soon gave me to know I had nothing to dread.

The poem was eventually published and quickly became popular around the United States. Unlike the European Saint Nicholas who was to be feared by naughty boys and girls, Moore's St. Nick was quite good-natured and fun.

In the 1860s, a cartoonist named Thomas Nast drew pictures of Santa Claus for the illustrated Harper's Weekly. It was there that his image as a plump and kindly old elf was immortalized.

The Santa Claus most familiar to us today was provided

by the Coca-Cola Company. In 1930, artist Fred Mizen painted a department store Santa in a crowd drinking a bottle of Coke. The jolly old elf with the white beard and dressed in a red suit laughed gregariously as his belly "shook like a bowl full of jelly."

VONETTA FLOWERS

Vonetta Flowers became the first African American to win a gold medal in the history of the winter Olympics. But Flowers did not always think of herself as a winner. In fact, Flowers never even imagined she would compete in the Winter Olympics. Flowers, a college All-American track and field athlete, had hoped to compete in the summer games. Though she made it into the trials, she failed to make the team.

Later, when the Women's National Bobsledding team conducted trials in her area, Flowers tried out on a whim. Remarkably, she placed second and veteran bobsled driver, Bonnie Warren, invited her to Germany to learn the sport.

Flowers was paired with Warren as a push-woman and they began training for the 2002 Winter Olympics. But several months before the trials, Warren unexpectedly replaced Flowers with a more seasoned athlete. Flowers was heartbroken. Without a driver, she had no chance of competing.

But fate stepped in: Jill Bakken needed a new push-woman. Flowers teamed up with her and began training anew for the Olympics. It was a long shot. Other teams were far better, but Bakken and Flowers focused on doing their absolute best. "We knew the importance of staying together and having faith in each other," said Bakken. That faith paid off when the underdog team achieved victory as the first Americans in over forty-six years to win a medal for the United States in bobsledding.

MAYBE SO, MAYBE NOT

There once was a village that had among its people a very wise man. The villagers trusted this man to provide them with answers to many of their questions. One day, a farmer from the village went to the wise man and said in a frantic tone, "Wise Man, help me. A horrible thing has happened. My ox has died and I have no animal to help me plow my field. Isn't this the worst thing that could have possibly happened?"

The wise old man replied, "Maybe so, maybe not."

The man hurried back to the village and reported to his neighbors the wise man had gone mad. Surely this was the worst thing that could have happened. Why couldn't the wise man see this?

The very next day, however, a strong young horse was seen near the man's farm. Because the man had no ox to rely on, he had the idea to catch the horse to replace his ox, and he did. With the help of the horse, plowing the field had never been easier. He went back to the wise man to apologize. "You were right, Wise Man. Losing my ox wasn't the worst thing that could have happened. It was a blessing in disguise. I never would have captured my new horse had I not lost my ox. You must agree that this is the best thing that could have happened."

The wise man replied once again, "Maybe so, maybe not."

Not again, thought the farmer. Surely the wise man has gone mad for sure.

But the farmer did not know the future. A few days later the farmer's son was riding the horse and was thrown off. He broke his leg and would not be able to help with the crop. "Oh no," thought the man, "now we will starve to death."

Once again the farmer went to the wise man. This time he said, "How did you know that capturing my horse was not a good thing? You were right again. My son is injured and won't be able to help with the crop. This time I'm sure that this is the worst thing that could have possibly happened. Surely you agree with me this time."

But just as he had done before, the wise man calmly looked at the farmer and with a compassionate tone said once again, "Maybe so, maybe not."

Enraged the wise man could be so stupid, the farmer stormed back to the village. The next day, troops arrived to take every able-bodied man away to war to serve the purposes of an evil king. The farmer's son was the only young man in the village who didn't have to go. He would live while the others would likely die.

GLENN CUNNINGHAM

After suffering burns on his legs at the age of five, Glenn Cunningham's doctors gave up. They believed he would be unable to walk for the balance of his life. Glenn would simply need to adjust to life in a wheelchair. "He will never be able to walk again," they said, "no chance."

The doctors examined his legs, but they had no way of looking into Glenn Cunningham's heart. He did not listen to the doctors. He resolved to walk again. Lying in bed, his skinny, red legs covered with scar tissue, Glenn vowed, "Next week, I am going to get out of bed. I am going to walk." And he did just that.

His mother tells of how she used to push back the curtain and look out the window to watch Glenn reach up and take hold of an old plow in the yard. With a hand on each handle, he began to make his gnarled and twisted legs function. And at every step, a step of pain, he came closer to walking. Soon he began to trot. Before long, he was running. When he started to run, he became even more determined. "I always believed that I could walk, and I did. Now I am going to run faster than anybody has ever run."

And did he ever! He became a great miler, who, in 1934, set a world's record of four minutes, six seconds. That same year, he was honored as the outstanding athlete of the century at Madison Square Garden. Glenn's ultimate goal was to "break the four minute barrier" and become the first person to run a mile in less than four minutes. While Glenn did not reach his ultimate goal, his story inspired a young medical student, Roger Bannister. In 1954, Bannister achieved the goal he shared with Glenn Cunningham; twenty years after Cunningham, the "boy who would never walk again" set a world record for the mile.

AN AFTERNOON IN THE PARK

There once was a little boy who wanted to meet God. He knew it was a long trip to where God lived, so he packed his suitcase with Twinkies and a couple of root beers and started his journey.

When he had gone about three blocks, he met an old woman. She was sitting in the park just staring at some pigeons. The boy sat down next to her and opened his suitcase. He was about to take a drink from his root beer when he noticed that the old lady looked hungry, so he offered her a Twinkie.

She gratefully accepted it and smiled. Her smile was so pretty the boy wanted to see it again, so he offered her a root beer. Once again she smiled at him and the boy was delighted. They sat there all afternoon eating and smiling, but they never said a word. As it grew dark, the boy realized how tired he was and he got up to leave. Before he had gone more than a few steps, he turned around, ran back to the old woman, and gave her a hug. She gave him her biggest smile ever.

When the boy opened the door to his house a short time later, his mother was surprised by the look of joy on his face. She asked him, "What did you do today that made you so happy?"

He replied, "I had lunch with God." But before his mother could respond, he added, "You know what? She's got the most beautiful smile I've ever seen!"

Meanwhile, the old woman, also radiant with joy, returned to her home. Her son was stunned by the look of peace on her face and he asked, "Mother, what did you do today that made you so happy?"

She replied, "I ate Twinkies in the park with God." But before her son responded, she added, "You know, he's much younger than I expected."

THE POWER OF WORDS

Words are powerful. They can inspire hope and they can destroy dreams. They can start a war, or heal a heart. The great baseball player Jackie Robinson had firsthand experience with the power of words. When he signed with the Brooklyn Dodgers, Robinson became the first African American to play major league baseball. He also became the target of racist hate mail and death threats. Prior to one game, Robinson received a threatening phone call that left him visibly shaken and unable to concentrate on the game. The caller had pushed him to his breaking point. He struck out in one inning with bases loaded. In another inning, he committed a fielding error and the crowd screamed obscenities at him. This was the worst day of his career.

A time out was called. His teammate, Pee Wee Reese, approached Robinson on the field. Reese put his arm around Robinson in front of the whole crowd and said, "Jackie, let me tell you something. I believe in you. You're the greatest baseball player I have ever seen. You can do it. I know that and I know something else. One of these days you are going to be in the Baseball Hall of Fame. So hold your head up high and play ball like only you can do it."

Robinson was heartened by those words and went on to deliver the game-winning hit for his team. Robinson recalled that incident many years later when he was inducted into the

Baseball Hall of Fame. He said of Pee Wee Reese, "He saved my life and my career that day. I had lost my confidence and Pee Wee picked me up with his words of encouragement. He gave me hope when hope was gone."

AN ACT OF CONGRESS

Irwin Rosenberg, a junior Naval officer, was discharged from military service after he was diagnosed with cancer, a standard military procedure at the time. The loss of his job was quite a blow, but he was determined to get back both his health and his job. With faith and dogged determination, he battled the disease that tried to take over his body. At one point, he was given only two weeks to live. But eventually, his cancer was brought under control.

Irwin then focused his attention on his desire to become a Naval officer. He discovered, however, that regulations forbade the reinstatement of a person discharged with cancer. Everyone told Irwin, "Give up. It would take an Act of Congress to get reinstated."

Their advice gave him an idea. He would pursue an Act of Congress. President Harry Truman eventually signed into law a special bill allowing Irwin Rosenberg to reenlist. He would eventually become a Rear Admiral serving in the United States Seventh Fleet.

Rear Admiral Irwin Rosenberg is confident he was both cured of cancer and reinstated in the U.S. Navy due to the "fervent prayers of God's people everywhere."

NOT HOME YET

On their way home from a lifetime of service as missionaries in Africa, an elderly couple found themselves on the same ocean liner as President Theodore Roosevelt, who was returning from a big game hunting expedition. The couple watched in awe at the fanfare given the President and his entourage. When the ship docked in New York, the band was waiting to greet him, the mayor was there to welcome him, and the newspapers hailed his return.

Meanwhile, the missionary couple slipped quietly off the ship and found an inexpensive apartment. They had no pension, they were in poor health, and they were discouraged and fearful. The husband, especially, could not seem to get over how President Roosevelt had received such acclaim, while their decades of service had gone without notice or reward. "God isn't treating us fairly," he complained bitterly to his wife.

"Why don't you pray about it," his wife advised.

A short time later, the wife noticed a change in her husband's demeanor. "What happened?" she asked.

The man replied, "The Lord put his hand on my shoulder and simply said, 'You're not home yet.'"

THE HABIT OF PRAYER

A surgeon in a large city hospital had a habit of insisting on a few minutes alone before he performed an operation. He had an outstanding reputation as a surgeon. One of the young physicians who worked with him wondered if there might be a correlation between his unusual habit and his unprecedented success. To the young doctor's inquiry, the surgeon answered, "Yes, there's a relationship. Before each operation, I ask the *Great Physician* to be with me, to guide my hands in their work. There have been times when I didn't know what to do next in the surgery, and then came the power to go on, power I knew came from God. I would not think of performing an operation without asking for His help."

The surgeon's words quickly spread through the hospital and then across the country. One day, a father brought his daughter to the hospital, insisting that the only doctor he would allow to touch her was the one who worked with God. When questioned about his preference, the father responded: "A surgeon willing to follow the manufacturer's handbook has to be a good surgeon."

A LITTLE FAITH

The temporary Sunday school teacher was struggling to open a combination lock on the minister's supply cupboard. She thought that perhaps she had forgotten the correct combination, so she went to the study and asked for help.

The minister came into the room and began to turn the dial. After the first two numbers, he paused and stared blankly for a moment. Then he lifted his eyes upward and whispered something too faint to the heard. He finally turned back to the lock, entered the final number, and opened it.

The teacher was amazed. "I'm in awe at your faith, pastor," she said.

"It's really nothing," he answered. "the number is taped to the ceiling."

One-Minute Lessons

Spark!

THE CODE

Insights from the Front Lines of Leadership

1. When a leader takes the high road, granting courtesy and consideration to those who withhold it, the best employees are comforted and reassured, the poorest employees annoyed. The best employees admire the high road, and, as a consequence, the leader who takes it. The best employees applaud the best of human behavior. They know the difficulty of being a good person in a bad circumstance. Take the high road, and listen for the quiet applause. It's out there.

2. An effective leader will not shun the use of authority when the situation demands it, but will avoid creating situations where use of authority is the only recourse. Building relationships with your team creates connections which allow you to limit the use of authority. "Because I do" is more effective than "because I said so."

3. Listening is the most effective motivational strategy leaders can practice. It is also the most neglected. Listening is personal; it builds mutual trust, demonstrates respect and creates a connection. It is the simplest way to say to another human being, "I care."

4. When managing conflict, focus on turning heat into light. Attack the issue or behavior, not the person. Give

all parties a hearing. Look for common ground. Work toward a solution everyone can adopt. If winning is your primary objective, prepare to lose your long-term relationships. True leadership creates win-win outcomes for everyone.

5. Telling the truth with compassion is always the best course. People deserve the truth regardless of any temporary pain it may cause them. If you are unwilling to share the hard truths, thereby withholding information vital to the success of another, you have abdicated your moral responsibility as a leader. You do not have the right to undermine the success of another human being.

6. As a leader, you are not paid to take risks. You are paid to know which risks are worth taking. The difference between success and extinction is knowledge, not daring. Your first priority is to insure survival of the company; the second is to secure profit.

7. Capable leaders are, first and foremost, simply capable of caring. No amount of education and experience can match the power of courtesy, empathy, and patience to bring out the best in people. Let the golden rule be your rule of thumb. Acknowledge those around you by name, whether they are cleaning the floor or presenting on it. Be sensitive to the feelings of others. Use words like "please" and "thank you" often. Common courtesy is not as common as it should be. Lead others to reverse this trend through your consistent courteous behavior.

8. Everyone has a heart they would gladly give to an organization where they know they matter. The human heart is the fountainhead of motivation, creativity, and innovation. Are you creating the environment where your team is contributing their heart as well as their mind?

9. Excellence is an appropriate goal. Perfectionism is not. Human behavior is not and never will be perfect regardless of your exhaustive efforts. Perfectionists seldom affirm others because they never affirm themselves.

10. Remember "The Emperor's New Clothes?" If only a caring courtier had told the Emperor in private what a small boy was willing to say so publicly! Show others you care by being honest about what you see. Your willingness to give others feedback shows them you want them to succeed. Treating them like adults who can handle the truth exhibits respect. Being candid isn't always easy, but don't let your failure lead to theirs. Set people up to succeed by sharing with them what you see, and encourage them to do the same for you.

11. Leaders help others become their best by helping others see themselves as the best. The words of those we respect make a difference in the way we see ourselves. Leaders know a well-intentioned person will improve quicker through praise than criticism. Words have weight. Leaders use words to grow not crush employees.

12. Our humanity ensures that we will make mistakes, but it should never be justification for letting mistakes go uncorrected. Patience with the mistakes of others does not equate to passivity. Mistakes are often the best learning opportunities, but only if those making the mistakes are made aware of them, shown how to correct them, and taught how to avoid them in the future. Leaders know that confronting a mistake today means avoiding an even bigger one tomorrow.

13. Leaders know the value of laughter. Human beings are a source of infinite amiable humor. Leaders anticipate the moment someone laughs at something they've said

or done. The wise leader laughs along with everyone else. Laughing at one's self demonstrates humility and confidence. It is evidence of being "comfortable in one's own skin," and therefore able to enjoy a good joke as much as anyone.

14. Leaders know that the path to excellence passes through the proverbial "briar patch." Knowing what is not so excellent about one's leadership style is key. Excellence requires direct reports willing and free to tell the boss the truth. Leaders reward honest feedback with an honest hearing and a genuine *thanks*.

15. Some clichés are true. For example: No one is perfect. Given that obvious insight, leaders know accountability will have to do. Accountability means the employee owns the mistake, corrects the mistake, learns from the mistake, and moves on; no handwringing as there's work to be done. Leaders know this is the path to continuous improvement.

16. Leaders choose their attitude. Leaders have an intrinsic understanding that while we cannot always choose what happens, we can choose our response. Leaders know that to remain positive in the face of adversity and disappointment signals a refusal to accept defeat. Such optimism strengthens and renews the efforts of the entire team.

17. Leaders value integrity. Integrity has been defined as the reputation earned with others. It means doing the right thing, regardless of the personal consequences, even when no one is watching. Leaders who are consistently loyal to the truth improve their reputation with others and with themselves.

18. Leaders embrace differences without assigning a value of better or worse to the experiences of others. Every life lens brings value to the team. A leader learns from the experience of others and celebrates their synergistic contribution to the team.

19. Leaders tell themselves the truth. Experience has taught them a dogged commitment to reality. Leaders know self-deception is the first step on the path to professional self-destruction.

20. A leader knows that a decision is not an action. The best ideas without feet travel nowhere. In a timely manner, leaders act on their decisions before the opportunity is lost.

21. An effective leader is also an active member of the team. Listening to employees and experiencing first-hand the work they do and the challenges they face puts the leader in a position to better understand what the team needs. The leader who is actively interested is more likely to act in the team's best interest.

22. Leaders know that they have been the beneficiary of another's generosity: advice, guidance, encouragement, mentoring. The best leaders pass it forward. Leaders give others the best of what they have been given.

23. The person most likely to get hurt on the job is experienced and well trained. They know what to do and how to do it. They've had extensive safety training and most of the time they follow safe work practices. The person most likely to get hurt on the job is someone just like your co-worker. Do you have his back?

24. Organizational productivity begins with effective leaders. When leaders do their jobs to the best of their abilities and help others to do the same, it makes it easier for the company to issue paychecks to everyone. Leaders know their positive impact on the bottom line has a positive impact for the entire organization.

25. Leaders master the art of patience. Impatience breeds fear, discouragement, and failure. Leaders know patience creates confidence, decisiveness, and a rational outlook which, given time, leads to success.

26. Good leaders know the best safety records are built at the speed of trust. When employees know they can give and receive safety feedback without paying a price, they will do so without hesitation. Leaders know a safe workplace depends on the team's emotional safety with each other.

27. Leaders go the second mile. Going the first mile is doing nothing more than what is required us. Leaders know it is in the second mile where excellence is achieved. Only the second mile [or third] reveals the best players/employees.

28. Leaders know that the most responsible thing a tired person can do is rest. Rest and begin again is a strategy for success. The best leaders know when to get busy and when to stop for at least a little while.

29. Encouraging others is easy when they are at their best. The best leaders encourage others in their worst moments as well. Leaders listen, talk through lessons learned and in doing so, point others to better performance.

30. Leaders know the best work processes and equipment are only as good as the relationships of the people

who run them. That's where *The Speed of Trust* adds efficiency. *The Speed of Trust* quickens the flow of ideas and thus, problem resolution. The best leaders earn trust while demonstrating a low tolerance for trust-busting behaviors.

31. Ensuring an ethical organization does not require a watchdog mentality, but dogged accountability. Set clear expectations for results, make clear the ethical parameters people must work within, and then hold them accountable for both. Allow people to work in their own ways to get results as long as they do not harm others. Leaders know they will get the ethical behavior they want by treating people like the adults they are.

32. Helping employees reach their full potential requires daily deposits of coaching and encouragement. Invest in your people by listening openly to ideas, praising honest efforts, and expressing confidence in their abilities. Leaders bank on these behaviors to yield dividends in employee performance.

33. Leaders know the truth of Yogi Berra's famous statement: "You can observe a lot by watching." Management by walking around (MBWA) has merit. Leaders know the value of just taking a casual stroll around their facility.

34. A leader is thankful and expresses gratitude for her team. She understands that she cannot do her job alone: she and the team must work together. A leader knows that humans want to be valued, not just for what they "do," but for the fact that they "are." An effective leader is not only thankful for the big successes, but for the small contributions made by each team member.

35. A leader values diversity and knows that each person has a unique life lens full of experience including joy, sorrow, accomplishment, failure, inspiring mentors, and harmful foes. A leader understands each idea brought to the table pushes the team toward one superior idea. Diversity in the team introduces new ideas, new perspectives, and new energy.

36. Leaders know that one of the best ways to "reward" a good employee is to ensure he or she is surrounded by other good employees. Those that work hard at building the *Speed of Trust* should get to work with trustworthy team members. Those that demonstrate a commitment to "getting results" should get to work with others who want to add value. Leaders are protectors of the common good.

37. *Change is hard* is an old but true cliché. Leaders know change is a present and future constant. Listening without judgment as an employee adjusts to changing circumstance and connecting them to reality (the facts of the situation) is a wise strategy. What an employee does with the considerate "ear" and "reality check" is up to them.

38. Upon hearing of his reported death, Mark Twain famously commented, "Rumors of my demise are greatly exaggerated." Leaders know that "saying it's so, don't make it so!" An opinion can be as unqualified as a rumor. And, an opinion can carry the gravitas of knowledge, experience, and wisdom. Leaders know the difference.

39. The great American humorist, Will Rogers, once commented that, "Nothing is more uncommon than common sense." Leaders know the obvious is not always obvious. Just because something "makes sense" to me,

does not mean it "makes sense" to everyone. Leaders know when to make common sense a bit more common.

40. Leaders know the experienced employee is the most "at risk" employee. It is human nature that the more you do something and the more you do it well, the more likely you are to place it below the level of awareness. Once complacency arrives, unsafe behaviors soon follow. Leaders know the path to safety is a continuous journey.

41. An effective leader appreciates the value of example: "I am already doing what I ask you to do." She understands when her walk matches her talk, her influence with the team increases. For example, a leader who wants a health-conscious team makes healthy choices. An effective leader expects nothing of her team that she is unwilling to do herself.

42. Leaders embrace change because they know opportunity resides within every change. Without change, there would be no prospect for growth, development, or advancement. Leaders help others accept change and grow through it.

43. "Life is long enough if you know what to do with it," said Seneca. To paraphrase: Leaders know the day is long enough if you know what to do with it. Time management is priority management. Wise leaders don't try to do everything. They do what is particularly important on a particular day.

44. Wherever people gather, gossip is the norm and the work place is no exception. Leaders do not talk about people. Leaders know that gossip hurts the object of the gossip and the perpetrator.

45. Choosing what is clearly right earns the respect of others. However, the decisions a leader has to make frequently have no clearly right or clearly wrong choices. When a leader has already earned the respect of others by making the clear choices, he will be trusted when he has to work in the gray areas.

46. A good and decent man offered this advice: Make your life your argument. Among leaders, it is a shared wisdom because leaders know what I say and how I say it and what I do and how I do it will always be my most convincing argument.

47. Past success may not lead to future success. The future will belong to innovation. Leaders encourage their team to challenge the status quo. Leaders know it is the best way to leapfrog the competition.

48. Saying what needs to be said, when it needs to said, in the manner in which it needs to be said, makes a leader vulnerable: vulnerable to the assertion of not caring about employees. Leaders know the best caring is telling the difficult truth with compassion.

49. Hydrangeas are my favorite flower. I especially enjoy the various shades you can achieve by manipulating the soil chemistry. Leaders know just as the level of pH in the soil impacts the color of a hydrangea bloom, a leader's attention to their team impacts individual performance. One team member may need a quiet "attaboy" while another team member may need public recognition.

50. The best leaders refuse to give destructive behavior a stage. They call a brief intermission, deal with the behavior in private, and then get back to business.

Leaders know that inappropriate behavior left unchecked eventually brings down the house.

51. The team member who needs constructive feedback the most usually pushes back the hardest. Leaders firmly provide constructive feedback regardless of pushback. It is the right thing to do.

52. Rationalization is the number one enemy of both safety and integrity. It is self-deception incognito. The courageous leader stands guard against the coward within who wants to talk him out of the right decision and into the easy one.

53. It's nice to be important. It's more important to be nice. Leaders know civility is a sign of character, not a sign of weakness.

54. We cannot control all of the changes that occur in our lives, but we can choose to grieve constructively through them. A leader knows he has to let go of what was in order to reach for the opportunity that will be.

55. Leaders value a post mortem, but they value a pre-mortem more. Examining what happened after the fact can be helpful. However, carefully thinking a decision through in advance is more helpful. A pre-mortem asks at least two questions: What is the worst-case scenario? And, if need be, can we live with it? Leaders know the best plan includes a plan for a failed plan.

56. As temperatures rise, so do tempers. Leaders know the value of a "time out." They take time outs and encourage their team to do the same. A cooling-off period can provide relief from the weather and stress. This simple

strategy, along with hydration, helps everyone keep their cool.

57. Our safety hinges on the questions, observations, and concerns of others. Leaders actively seek fresh perspectives and different approaches. They know what they don't know can hurt them.

58. Leaders recognize the value of trust and build it within their team at every opportunity. Their toolbox is equipped with candor, fairness, predictability, transparency, integrity, and competence. Construction is continuous. It's not possible to overbuild.

59. The conventional wisdom in management is getting things done through people. Not a bad definition, as far as it goes. Leaders know the wiser course is to develop people through work.

60. Leaders know conversation is an opportunity to improve a relationship. Hearing people out involves our eyes as well as our ears. Tone, volume, and body language say more than the words people use. When a leader "sees" the whole story being told, others see the leader's interest in hearing more.

61. Leaders create a good day for those around them with their positive spirit, their sense of purpose, and their decisive actions. Leaders don't leave a good day to chance; they choose to make it happen. Make today a great day for your team.

62. We are, through the pattern of our behavior, either giving others permission to keep us safe or, warning them to tread carefully when alerting us to a safety concern.

Leaders know the more grateful we are for someone's concern, the more likely they are to keep us safe.

63. Team members love change when they initiate the change. Unfortunately, most of us spend a good part of our work life making our way through change we did not initiate. Leaders know times of change do more than develop character; they also reveal character.

64. The nature of change is it produces fear, including fear of losing the familiar and fear of the new and unknown. So change requires courage. Leaders know that courage is not the absence of fear. It is the recognition that something is more important than fear.

65. The biggest and best ideas can be shot down by people with the smallest minds. In spite of this fact, leaders know they have to generate bigger and better ideas.

66. Sometimes there is only a fleeting moment to offer words to support an employee, to comfort a friend, or to encourage a child. When the moment is missed, it is often lost forever. Leaders embrace the opportunity. They choose their words carefully, but never leave important words unsaid.

67. Leaders know doing what you love means dealing with things you don't love. And, the failure to deal with what you don't love will, sooner or later, prevent you from doing what you love.

68. Leaders know and live trust: Do what is right. Deliver what is promised. Be the same person, whatever the circumstances. Be accountable. Leaders build trust by being trustworthy.

69. Leaders know it is in knowing the past that we alter the future. Doing it the way we've always done it will not produce a different result. Different outcomes spring from different behaviors.

70. Leaders understand people matter. Even when a team member requires guidance or a reprimand, a leader remembers the team member's value and treats him in a way which affirms his value.

71. Leaders do what needs to be done, when it needs to be done, whether they feel like it or not. They are not so much men and women of steel as they are people others can count on. No hedging. No excuses. No complaints.

72. When deadlines are looming and economic storms are raging, a leader walks toward the difficulty. Walking a team through challenging times requires a leader who takes the first step. Courage and confidence are best instilled by a courageous, confident example.

73. Leaders know the power of passion. Caring passionately whittles the world down to a more manageable size. It places the spotlight on what can be done, rather than on what cannot. Leaders make things happen.

74. Leaders trust themselves. They know what they know; and, they know what they don't know. They are honest with themselves about both. They know when to leverage their knowledge and experience. And, they know when to leverage the knowledge and experience of others.

75. Leaders know fear causes people to do the quick and easy thing. Leaders face and manage their fears. Even when alarmed on the inside, leaders keep a steady hand on the task at hand.

76. Mark Twain offered the following advice to an aspiring writer: When your work speaks for itself and says good things, don't interrupt. Leaders know the best argument is a job well done.

77. Leaders know the most difficult moment in any argument is the moment you realize you are wrong. Leaders are not driven by the need to *be right*. Leaders are driven by the need to *get it right*.

78. A well-balanced tire ensures a safer, smoother ride on even the bumpiest road. People, too, require emotional maintenance and a balanced life to handle life's occasional bumps. The best leaders encourage others to take time for the occasional tune-up.

79. Leaders know trust reduces cost and increases efficiency: the greater the trust, the higher the morale and productivity. The lower the trust, the longer it takes and the more everything costs. Leaders demonstrate trust, extend trust, and deal quickly with trustbusters.

80. Leaders know it is direction, not intent, that determines destination. My best thoughts are not my best ideas until they become a successfully executed plan. It is the difference between a plan and wishful thinking.

81. The best communicators know body language speaks volumes. When the reaction we see doesn't match the message we intended to communicate, it is a clear sign that it's time to listen. Ask the receiver to state back the message he heard to ensure it's the one you meant to send. Testing what we see by listening to what was heard ensures our messages are communicated—and received—as intended.

82. Leaders know planning is the difference between ready, aim, fire and ready, fire, aim! A carefully developed plan is not a guarantee. It does, however, tip the odds substantially in your favor.

83. Understanding that human performance is not perfect, a leader is patient with employees as they learn and grow. This patience is not without consequence. Although patient, a leader ensures accountability is a part of every relationship. People are expected to own their mistake, correct the mistake to the degree that they can, learn from the mistake, and move on.

84. It is often said that wisdom comes with age. It has been my observation that age sometimes comes alone. Not everyone "grows up" on the preferred timetable. An employee can be old (as in wise) when young. An employee can be young (as in immature) when old. Take the time to consider the ideas of your youngest employees. When necessary, do not hesitate to "mentor" the employee who is older than you.

85. Not everyone believes they need the goodwill of others. There is always the employee who thinks they know everything and can do anything. Then there is the confident, but humble employee who has learned through life's lessons there is much to learn from others. They welcome what others bring to the table. They know the value of goodwill. Don't waste your mental energy on the know-it-all. You cannot teach someone who has nothing new to learn. Focus instead on encouraging the good and decent people who are working hard at getting better.

86. Leaders understand the greatest courtesy they can extend to their team is to speak the truth about performance. Leaders avoid falling into the trap of misplaced

compassion; hurting a person long-term by failing to tell them a helpful truth. Leaders know the human need to make sense out of things requires that team members know where they stand.

87. It is a fool's errand to try to make perfect what was never meant to be perfect: human performance. There are no perfect employees or organizations. The good news is our quirks and eccentricities can add interest, even fun, to a work day. The bad news? We rarely look more foolish than when we demand flawless performance from ourselves or others. The wise leader settles for accountability: the employee who owns a mistake, corrects a mistake, learns from a mistake (i.e. continuous improvement), and moves on with no hand-wringing. There's work to be done!

88. The best leaders are also teachers. They share their life experiences with others and mentor them to reach their highest potential. Effective mentors begin by building mutual trust. They know we learn most easily from those whom we trust to look out for our best interests. Leaders know learning is a life-long journey best travelled at the speed of trust.

89. A diamond-cutter begins with an understanding the rough diamond is already valuable. His job is to cut the diamond along its natural shape; minimizing flaws and enhancing its natural brilliance and color to reach its maximum potential value. In the same way, effective mentors identify early the natural talents and abilities of their team members. Then they carefully chip away at the rough edges to clarify the brilliance that already exists. Mentors understand as each individual shines brighter, the organization as a whole becomes more valuable.

90. A life well lived is lived in service to others. We exist temporarily through what we take, but live forever through what we give. Leaders serve. Leaders point others to something larger than themselves.

91. The higher the leader is in the organization, the more reluctant others are to risk the leader's displeasure by voicing a dissenting opinion or sharing bad news. Leaders know the value of receiving candid and timely input. A leader's success may well depend on how safe an employee feels speaking truth to power.

92. There's a reason the flight attendant wants you to put the oxygen mask on yourself first: you can't help others if you're unconscious. Leaders know taking care of others means taking care of themselves first! Proper rest, a healthy diet, daily exercise, and a strong dose of laughter are essential strategies for good self-maintenance. Taking care of one's self, emotionally and physically, ensures the strength and endurance to guide others.

93. Leaders understand the value of being present. Leaders focus on the person at hand. While distractions are inevitable, the best leaders put down their phones, turn away from their computers, and turn their full attention to the person(s) standing in front of them.

94. Processes can't be too efficient and profits can't be too high. People can't be too safe. A leader knows that continuous safety, like continuous improvement, requires continuous conversation.

95. Most team members have tasks they enjoy more than others. They rarely assess the continued value of what they like doing. Leaders know the value of a task is dynamic and ever-changing. Team members add value

not only through what they do, but through what they stop doing when it no longer adds value.

96. Leaders seek wise counsel rather than sympathetic commiseration. They know constructive feedback offered with compassion is more valuable than solicitous approval. Leaders appreciate those who are willing to tell them what they need to hear, however painful it may be. They recognize truth-telling as an investment in their success.

97. Leaders know complacency is the thief lurking around the edges of safety, compliance, and success. Proactive conversations reinforce diligence and keep the thief at bay.

98. Anybody with money to burn will easily find someone to tend the fire. Leaders know a poorly managed budget is an invitation to a five-alarm fire. Stewardship is an obligation of leadership.

99. Leaders know you can often tell more about a person by what they say about others than you can by what they say about themselves. Leaders listen for an earned compliment. They also listen for the *put down* which is merely self-serving.

100. The stage and screen actor, Andy Griffith said, "Worry is like a rocking chair, it will give you something to do, but it won't get you anywhere." Leaders are, by their nature, *going somewhere*. They view the temptation to *worry* as a reminder to get busy doing *what can be done—* whatever the circumstances.

101. Leaders know the world is not black and white. Ambiguity and uncertainty are often present. Leaders push past

analysis paralysis. Leaders make timely decisions based on the best information available.

102. Viktor Frankl said, "When we no longer can change a situation, we are challenged to change ourselves." Leaders know they are not powerless. They know they can always change themselves in order to meet the challenge ... or to rise above it.

103. Leaders are quick to learn from the mistakes of others. They know they can't possibly live long enough to make all the mistakes themselves!

104. *There is no need in telling other people your troubles because half don't care and the other half are glad you've got them.* While never cynical, leaders *are* discreet in what they say and to whom they say it.

105. Some people believe: *It's all about who you know, not what you know.* In reality, that is rarely true. We don't ask the dentist next door to be our mechanic just because we know him. It is human nature to want to work with people we know. Even so, leaders know competence, trust, and respect must trump *merely* knowing someone.

106. When all the contents of a canoe are placed on one side, the canoe flips. Leaders balance all aspects of their lives so that when navigating the work day, they are able to focus on the work at hand, rather than the unbalanced contents of their canoe.

107. Leaders know they can earn trust by first giving it away. They extend trust to others before it is earned. When others sense you trust them, they will often rise to meet your expectations; and in the process, will trust you for having first trusted them.

108. Benjamin Whichcote said, "None are so empty as those who are full of themselves." Leaders know *I* is a smaller word than *we*. They evaluate what they hear accordingly.

109. People cannot trust someone they do not know. A leader recognizes to build the speed of trust she must reveal enough of herself to make others feel comfortable. Through human connection, trust is forged and through character, it is sustained.

110. Leaders know you can stand tall without standing on someone. Leaders know anyone who has to knock others down in order to feel tall will never be tall enough to lead. You can be a victor without having victims. Leaders value accountability, not casualties.

111. Industrialist Henry J. Kaiser said, "When your work speaks for itself, don't interrupt." Leaders know when to speak up and when to keep their own counsel. If the work product doesn't speak for itself, there's little you can add which will make a difference.

112. Leaders do not dwell on mistakes; they learn from mistakes. They recognize the potential for human error and minimize the likelihood of error. However, leaders know that no one is perfect. When mistakes happen, leaders focus on the opportunity to learn and grow.

113. A leader will *own* being wrong. It is just another way of saying "I'm wiser today than I was yesterday."

114. According to an old Venezuelan adage, "If you're going to hunt a bullfrog, don't use a shotgun." Leaders know blowing up little issues loudly and openly can be more than just messy. The result will be big damage with

little benefit. A *rifle shot is far better*—focused, specific, logical, face to face, without an audience.

115. Leaders think in terms of "I can," not "I can't." Leaders set realistic goals, use what they know, learn what they don't know, and pair it with a positive attitude to get the job done.

116. Economist Thomas Sowell said, "It takes considerable knowledge just to realize the extent of your own ignorance." Leaders limit their ignorance by listening at least as much as they talk.

117. A leader knows he must choose his words carefully. Once said, they can't be withdrawn and damage is not easily repaired. Thomas Jefferson once boasted, "One of my most prized possessions are words that I have never spoken." It's a measure of wealth worth building.

118. There are good reasons farmers don't keep their bulls in china shops. There are also good reasons why organizations don't keep bullies around. *Breaking good is not acceptable. Building good* means culling those who consistently damage team cohesion, no matter how technically competent they may be.

119. "Give a man a fish, feed him for a day. Teach a man to fish, feed him for a lifetime." is a popular Chinese proverb. Leaders teach others *to fish*. They do not deliver a fish when a fishing lesson is required.

120. Leaders know *the smartest guy in the room* will, in time, be *the most embarrassed guy in the room*. Nobody knows everything. A little humility is its own reward.

121. A New Year's Resolution: Rise above small things. Rise above the petty. Rise above the mean-spirited. Rise above tit-for-tat. Rise above the worst of human behavior. Rise above the noise of what matters least. Leaders rise!

122. Lighthouses were built to warn sailors of specific unseen dangers that would otherwise sink ships. A workplace too can have any number of hidden dangers. In the workplace, the lighthouse is open communication: an atmosphere where people at all levels will speak up and say what needs to be said, when it needs to be said, with no retribution for proactive truth telling. Hearing something unpleasant is far preferable to a fast, silent, and pleasant ride straight into a shipwreck.

123. As good as folk wisdom can be, leaders know the limits of folk wisdom. For example: We are often told we cannot change the world. The truth is the world is changing every day. The only question is who is doing the changing? Leaders are change agents—they change things for the better!

124. Sometimes the most courageous thing a leader does is tell herself the truth. Humans have an uncanny ability to *color the truth* to avoid pain or discomfort. Continuing to say, "I am my best self!" does not make it true. Looking at our behavior critically and soliciting feedback from those we trust takes courage. No matter how painful the truth, it is never as painful as a lie.

125. There is one guaranteed outcome to losing one's temper: lost respect. And nothing spreads faster than news of poor behavior. A wise leader knows the logical action to take in a maddening moment is to step away and regain composure. Thoughtful responses trump emotional reactions.

126. Young team members can't possibly have had all the experiences their leader may have had, but with time and thoughtful mentoring they will build their skill set to add great value to the team. A leader is patient while others learn and grow. She sees not only who the team member is today, but the potential of who they will become in the years ahead.

127. Leaders know the value of connecting with their team. The more connected team members feel, the better they behave and perform. The same holds true for leaders. Leaders who are connected to their team strive to be their best selves for the team's sake as well as their own. A ship's captain is more effective when in the boat rather than directing it from shore.

128. Leaders know the irony of human behavior is that we tend to run faster when we have lost our way. Leaders are thoughtful and methodical. Leaders run faster only by design—not by default.

129. During the Great Depression of the 1930s, the US Soil Conservation Service paid Southern farmers to plant a little known Japanese vine called kudzu. It was intended for erosion control. It does control erosion; it, in fact, controls everything it grows over. The runaway vine now dominates over seven million acres of former farmland that is no longer useable for row crops or forestland. A wise leader makes decisions conscious of likely impacts, knowing effects matter far more than good intentions alone.

130. When we think of Italian food, it is difficult not to think of tomatoes, especially in spaghetti sauce, lasagna, etc. But the tomato is native to the Americas, not Italy. Italian food was tomato-less until many years after Christopher

Columbus. Someone saw a possibility while someone else no doubt grumbled, "That's not how we do it here." Even where tradition is prized, a wise leader actively seeks to establish a workplace culture where new ideas are welcome.

131. In spite of the best possible plans, leaders are often faced with outcomes they couldn't have predicted and do not desire. At those moments, they embrace flexibility and adaptability. Disappointments and setbacks are inevitable. A leader knows a bend in the road is never the end of the road unless you fail to navigate the curve.

132. Leaders know that while we are only young once, immaturity can last a lifetime. Leaders can see maturity in the young and immaturity in the old—and understand the implications of both.

133. It is common for a member of a more seasoned generation to exaggerate, "It is a shame that young people don't talk to one another in person anymore—social media is destroying communication." If you talk to a younger person, they may well dramatically lament, "I can't believe the inefficient, outdated way older folks communicate with so few and do it so poorly." An effective leader is careful not to automatically buy into or to automatically dismiss generational biases without considering both perspectives.

134. Arby's president Hala Moddelmog said, "There is no substitute for being prepared, practiced, and knowledgeable." Good leaders are confident in what they know and are willing to put in the time and learn what they don't know.

135. Leaders live up to their highest opinions of themselves—quietly, unassumingly, even when no one is watching. At the end of the day, we usually know if we've been the person we wanted to be or if we've fallen short. Leaders assume responsibility for outcomes; no short-cuts, no complaints, and no excuses.

136. Leaders know those who love to complain can always find a gripe. And, those who wish to sing can always find a song. Leaders develop a chorus—they don't get lost in the background noise.

137. Leaders know work is a good thing. A task completed, a job well done, the personal satisfaction of excellent craftsmanship, the pride of achievement, demonstrating "I am up to the job" confirms the intrinsic human need to matter. Leaders value and demonstrate respect for work rightly done.

138. Leaders know it is impact not intent that builds or damages relationships. I may be well-intentioned, but others can only hear my words or see my actions. They cannot know what's in my mind or in my heart. A leader strives for impact which is consistent with intent and is quick to right any wrongs created by a gap between the two.

139. Nelson Mandela is quoted as saying, "What counts in life is not the mere fact that we have lived. It is what difference we have made to the lives of others that will determine the significance of the life we lead." Effective leaders seek to make a difference. They understand every moment of patience, every compassionate performance management conversation, every decision made for the common good is all part of a much bigger picture—investing in the lives of others!

140. Leaders know obsessing over a mistake is nothing more than an argument with the past. Leaders do not live in the past. They argue for and work for a better future.

141. It is not uncommon to see a handwritten thank you card which was written weeks or months prior still displayed in an office, cubicle, or workspace. During the interim time period, the person may have received hundreds of emails and texts which are displayed nowhere. A leader knows finding a way to make messages of genuine gratitude stand out is important.

142. During her time hiking the Pacific Crest Trail alone, Cheryl Strayed experienced moments of doubt and fear. She said, "Fear, to a great extent, is born of a story we tell ourselves, and so I chose to tell myself a different story from the one women are told. I decided I was safe. I was strong. I was brave. Nothing could vanquish me." Be bold. Evaluate whether the story you are telling yourself is working for you or against you.

143. "Dear George-Remember no man is a failure who has friends. Thanks for the wings.-Clarence." That was the note written to the main character in the classic movie *It's A Wonderful Life.* Often developing lasting friendships, most of us spend at least as much or more time with our co-workers as with our family members. Leaders recognize how important friendships in the workplace are to each person's overall well-being and even to their level of performance. Leaders know that workplace lunches and social opportunities have a great deal more meaning than just the meal itself.

144. A friend recently shared a simple reminder with me. "The first place we lose the battle is in our own thinking. If you think it's permanent, then it's permanent. If you

think you've reached your limits, then you have. If you think you'll never get well, then you won't. You have to change your thinking. You need to see everything that's holding you back, every obstacle, every limitation as only temporary." Leaders know our thinking impacts the outcome—for good or bad.

145. Exceptional results are seldom random. They are the product of consistent good judgment. A leader knows the choices made each day determine the life we construct, the health we enjoy, the relationships we build and the work we create. The difference is in the choosing.

146. Rumors spread around the workplace are often sensational. Despite the adage, smoke is not always accompanied by fire. When it comes to rumors, sometimes there is just a smoke screen of jealousy, insecurity, misinformation, or confusion. A leader separates rumor from truth, does not spread rumors, and holds accountable those who do.

147. The human brain's number one priority is to ensure the survival of its owner. Imagine—100,000,000,000 brain cells dedicated to your well-being! A leader protects this most valuable asset with a healthy diet, regular exercise, and adequate rest. Take care of your brain so it will continue to take care of you.

148. Leaders work to influence the outcomes they can, but recognize there are always things beyond their control. Some battles are not theirs to fight. By focusing on their sphere of influence, leaders spend their energy where they can make a difference.

149. It's a proven fact a leader with a balanced life is more productive over time. Total focus on one area can lead to stress, burn out, and agonizing disappointment. Balance

provides resilience and the opportunity for renewal. Attention to the Life Wheel keeps you rolling toward achievement of your goals.

150. My hometown is a place where all four seasons are enjoyed. Temperatures are beginning to drop, the Friday night football game can be heard clearly from my back porch, and leaves are beginning to fall around my house. As the seasons change, it reminds me change should be embraced. Change is the place where new ideas begin, process improvements occur and teams grow. Effective leaders embrace the opportunity change presents.

151. A leader knows the value of a positive attitude. You can't control the daily ups and downs, but you can choose how you react to them. A positive outlook and a belief you can handle any situation fuels self-confidence. Others are attracted to a confident, optimistic leader.

152. A local restaurant I frequent has a "Suggestion Box" hanging on a wall. Interestingly, it is made from Plexiglas, so I am able to see into the box. I am certain the same two pieces of folded paper have been in the box at least six months. Every time I see the box, it compels me to reflect on how often I ask for feedback or suggestions, yet give the impression I really do not want input from others. Effective leaders demonstrate they sincerely want feedback.

153. The Latin phrase *age quod agis* loosely translates, "work hard at what you do well." We've all been told at some time or another we should work on our opportunities for improvement. While it's important to minimize behaviors which may not serve us well, leaders know their strengths and work to enhance them. The great

philosopher Dolly Parton put it another way: "Find out who you are and do it on purpose."

154. Did someone in your past make a lasting impression on you? Is there someone who mentored you or invested in your success by sharing helpful feedback? If so, have you taken the time to thank them for the meaningful role they played? Consider this leadership challenge: Write a note today to someone who was influential in your success. An email or text does not qualify. It should be a hand-written note mailed the old-fashioned way. Leaders value relationships. They know relationships, whether personal or professional, make all the difference in a life well lived.

155. Leaders know it is not as important to know everything as to know the value of everything—*What is worth a leader's time* and *what is not? What has durable value and what does not?*

156. Listening is one of the least used strategies for building trust. Listening is caring and team members appreciate an empathetic hearing even when the circumstances can't be changed. Leaders know the value of listening.

157. Leaders know there is little difference in people, but that little difference makes a big difference. The little difference is attitude. The big difference is whether it is positive or negative.

158. Leaders understand the value of humor. Nothing cleanses the mind like a good belly laugh. Laughter releases endorphins, your body's natural pain relievers. Laughter has proven to lower blood pressure and reduce stress. Leaders take their job seriously, but not themselves.

The ability to laugh at oneself is a hallmark of a self-confident leader.

159. Leaders know the most difficult secret to keep is their opinion of themselves. Sooner or later, what leaders think of themselves will spill over into their treatment of others.

160. Leaders know you teach your team what is acceptable by what you allow, what you stop, and what you reinforce. Action provides clarity!

161. There's always a crowd willing to identify problems. Leaders stand out by proactively seeking solutions. They focus on ideas rather than complaints and never play the blame game.

162. Leaders have an obligation to dissent. Following consensus may be the comfortable thing to do, but there's a reason you're at the table. Your experience and expertise bring a unique perspective to your organization. Leaders value a different point of view and are always willing to contribute their own.

163. Leaders know every minute of every day counts. A moment of inattention or less than their best effort can be the difference between success and a close second place. Outcomes count, but so does knowing you put forth your best effort.

164. When Admiral Mike Mullen became Chairman of the Joint Chiefs of Staff, he recalls receiving this warning from his predecessor: "You'll eat some very good food, but be prepared never to hear the truth again." The higher the leader rises in the organization, the more reluctant others are to risk the leader's displeasure by voicing a

dissenting opinion or sharing bad news. Leaders know the value of receiving candid and timely input. A leader's success may well depend on how safe an employee feels speaking truth to power.

165. Leaders do not resign themselves to fate—they know their resignation is likely to be accepted. Leaders *think, plan, collaborate, decide* and *execute.*

166. Leaders know the wisdom found in want versus need. What is wanted is not necessarily what is needed. The best example is the way a whole day can slip away when you're deliberately avoiding what needs to be done.

167. Leaders know the problem is not that there are problems. The problem is expecting otherwise and thinking having problems is a problem. Problem solving is not merely normal. Problem solving refines a team's competence and confidence.

168. Leaders know self-improvement is impossible if your only model is yourself. The good example of another person provides a compass. Heroic stories of high principle and sacrificial service to the common good have a place in the workplace.

169. Leaders choose their attitude. Leaders have an intrinsic understanding that while we cannot always choose what happens, we can choose our response. Leaders know remaining positive in the face of adversity and disappointment signals a refusal to accept defeat. Such optimism strengthens and renews the efforts of the entire team.

170. Leaders know it is often easier to forgive others their mistakes than to forgive others for having witnessed

one's own mistakes. Leaders do not present themselves as perfect. Leaders present themselves as accountable.

171. Leaders provide encouragement. They provide encouragement for those who are struggling as well as for the effective team member. Leaders know positive reinforcement propels a team toward high performance. When a leader believes in the team, the team starts to believe in itself.

172. A man went to a psychiatrist and told him, "My brother needs help. He thinks he's an orange."
"That sounds serious," said the doctor. "I'll be happy to see him as soon as he makes an appointment."
"Well," said the man, "since the situation is urgent, I brought him along right here in my pocket."
Leaders know even those who present themselves as reasonable can be unreasonable. Leaders match words to behaviors in order to know reality.

173. As a young man, George Washington settled on 110 Rules of Civility and Decent Behavior which he followed throughout his life. Number six is as follows: Sleep not when others speak, sit not when others stand, speak not when you should hold your peace, walk not when others stop. Leaders know what Washington knew; civil behavior raises the bar for a team through a good example.

174. Fraud in the Insurance industry is calculated to be $150 billion a year, a cost that gets passed along to consumers in the form of higher premiums. Altogether, public and private-sector fraud costs every household in the United States around $5000 a year. Leaders know there are bad actors in this world. Leaders are neither naïve nor cynical. Leaders believe in what people can be at their

best while remaining alert to the bad actor hidden among the good.

175. Communities devastated by natural or man-made disasters often rise above the disruption and chaos. In the aftermath of Hurricane Katrina, small towns and crossroad communities across the Mississippi and Louisiana Gulf Coast witnessed the best of human behavior. Neighbor helped neighbor. The sharing of available food and water immediately became the norm—so much so that when state and federal assistance arrived they discovered communities already on their way to getting the proverbial ox out of the ditch. Leaders know the best team members help themselves before expecting the help of others.

176. Charlie Chaplin once lost a Charlie Chaplin look-alike contest. He failed to make even the top three. Leaders know *the obvious is not always obvious.* Leaders compensate by asking at least *a question or two* about their own assumptions.

177. Dr. Seuss wrote *Green Eggs and Ham* after his editor challenged him to produce a book using fewer than fifty different words. It took Theodore Geisel [a.k.a. Dr. Seuss] more than a year, working four to six hours a day. Leaders know it is far more difficult to be brief, concise and clear. Leaders know *simple is often profound.*

178. Leaders know when it comes to food for thought some people are on a hunger strike. The best leaders digest the new idea with the same objective palate with which they critique the old and familiar.

179. Henry Ford invented the modern charcoal briquette from sawdust and scrap wood generated in his automobile

Spark!

factory. Ford encouraged people to use their cars on picnic outings by offering barbecue grills and *Ford Charcoal* at his dealerships. Leaders are open to the possibility that what others call "scrap" may carry the seed of an innovative idea.

180. One twenty-fifth of the energy released by an incandescent lightbulb is light. The rest is heat. A typical LED bulb virtually reverses this light to heat ratio—an improvement which required years of thoughtful effort. Leaders know solutions which are "good enough" today must be improved upon for a sustainable tomorrow.

181. The sandbox tree grows pumpkin-shaped fruit that explodes when ripe. The explosion launches the seeds as far as 300 feet at speeds up to 150 mph. Its nickname is the "dynamite tree." Leaders know business, just like nature, often confronts us with the strange and unexpected. The best strategy for minimizing the dynamite tree effect is thoughtful planning.

182. In Japanese business culture, it is socially acceptable for an employee to fall asleep on the job. It is viewed as a sign that they have been working really hard. Leaders know when a team member should *rest and begin again*. An exhausted employee is an *at-risk* employee. A safe workplace is a workplace that respects the limits of human performance.

183. Leaders do not look back in anger or forward in fear. They look around in awareness. The past is the past. Opportunity lies ahead.

184. Leaders know leadership is a journey. Leaders know knowledge evolves, understanding matures, and wisdom progresses when you are open to learning the lessons of

life that work will teach. And, as often as not, the best lessons arrive packaged in discomfort.

185. Christopher Columbus always believed he had landed in Asia instead of in the "New World." Recent polls indicate one in four Americans believe the moon landing was a hoax. And, more than one-third of the US population believe crossing paths with a "black cat" is bad luck. Leaders are ever mindful of those who do not allow facts to get in the way of a good story.

186. Leaders know there is a great difference between worry and resolve. A worried person sees a problem. A resolute person solves a problem—not so much with ease, as with grit.

187. Leaders know the best solution seldom requires that someone be right and someone else be wrong. It is not enough to be right. Good ideas are not adopted automatically. They become common practice through courageous patience.

188. It's true no organization ever rises above its leadership. It's also true our organization can never be anything we do not want ourselves to be. Leaders know if they want excellence, compassion, truthfulness, or courage in the organization's culture, they must first find it within themselves.

Printed in the United States
By Bookmasters